Richard Henry Smith

Exposition of the Cartoons of Raphael

Richard Henry Smith

Exposition of the Cartoons of Raphael

ISBN/EAN: 9783337060121

Printed in Europe, USA, Canada, Australia, Japan

Cover: Foto ©ninafisch / pixelio.de

More available books at **www.hansebooks.com**

EXPOSITIONS

OF THE

CARTOONS OF RAPHAEL.

BY

RICHARD HENRY SMITH, Jun.

ILLUSTRATED BY PHOTOGRAPHS,

PRINTED BY NEGRETTI AND ZAMBRA.

LONDON:
JAMES NISBET AND CO., 21 BERNERS STREET.
M.DCCC.LXI.

PREFACE.

SOME years ago, the writer of the following "Expositions of the Cartoons of Raphael" began to study in the Gallery at Hampton Court, and found himself continually falling into conversation with the visitors who were constantly courting information about these great pictures. Becoming, year after year, more interested in the cartoons, as he became more familiar with them, he was led to search the Scriptures from which Raphael selected his subjects. The present book is the result of his investigation of the sacred record of the various scenes, and of his study of their treatment by this " divine "-painter.

There was no difficulty, in the very presence of the originals, to explain to *listeners* the bearing and force of his remarks. Seeing for themselves, they could exercise their own judgments, and receive or reject what he had to say. It will be as easy for *readers*, now photography has lent its aid, to judge for themselves the correctness of the various statements.*

The unexpected interest which has been manifested in these famous but neglected works, warrants the writer, in his conviction,

---

* The use of a glass will be sometimes a necessity, and will be always an advantage in the study of the photographs.

that they have only to be known to be appreciated. Till the publication of the photographs, the cartoons were hidden in the dark gallery at Hampton Court, and their unpopularity is greatly to be attributed to their unfortunate position. They have now been brought to the light, and they will commend themselves alike to new and old admirers.

Those who have never seen, and who are never likely to see, the cartoons, will be persuaded, from their knowledge of the fidelity of photography, that it may be safely trusted in a literal translation of the originals. Those who have often seen them will be induced, by the novelty of this version, to renew their acquaintance with the painter in his best works.

The profession will immediately detect the hand of a layman in the comments which accompany the illustrations. The writer is no more an artist than a photograph is a picture. He has sought to represent, in his own way, without any pretence, his conception of the purpose of Raphael in this series of Bible pictures. While fully aware of the sombreness of the tone of his expositions, and the comparative exaggeration in their chiaro-oscuro, the writer yet trusts that there may be found in them (as there are to be found in the photographs) some happy accidents, by which the existence and meaning of facts are so evidently set forth, that they can neither be unnoticed nor mistaken.

It is possible that it may be necessary to remind some that Raphael was not a pre-Raphaelite.

HAMPTON GROVE, SURBITON, S.W.
September 1860.

CONTENTS.

		PAGE
I.	THE MIRACULOUS DRAUGHT OF FISHES,	1
II.	THE CHARGE TO PETER,	16
III.	PETER AND JOHN HEALING THE LAME MAN AT THE BEAUTIFUL GATE OF THE TEMPLE,	23
IV.	THE DEATH OF ANANIAS,	39
V.	THE CONVERSION OF SERGIUS PAULUS,	51
VI.	PAUL AND BARNABAS REJECTING THE SACRIFICE AT LYSTRA,	63
VII.	PAUL PREACHING AT ATHENS,	77

THE CARTOONS OF RAPHAEL.

No. I.

The Miraculous Draught of Fishes.

"And it came to pass, that, as the people pressed upon him to hear the word of God, he stood by the lake of Gennesaret, and saw two ships standing by the lake: but the fishermen were gone out of them, and were washing their nets. And he entered into one of the ships, which was Simon's, and prayed him that he would thrust out a little from the land. And he sat down, and taught the people out of the ship. Now when he had left speaking, he said unto Simon, Launch out into the deep, and let down your nets for a draught. And Simon answering said unto him, Master, we have toiled all the night, and have taken nothing: nevertheless at thy word I will let down the net. And when they had this done, they inclosed a great multitude of fishes: and their net brake. And they beckoned unto their partners, which were in the other ship, that they should come and help them. And they came, and filled both the ships, so that they began to sink. When Simon Peter saw it, he fell down at Jesus' knees, saying, Depart from me; for I am a sinful man, O Lord. For he was astonished, and all that were with him, at the draught of the fishes which they had taken: and so was also James, and John, the sons of Zebedee, which were partners with Simon. And Jesus said unto Simon, Fear not; from henceforth thou shalt catch men. And when they had brought their ships to land, they forsook all, and followed him."—LUKE v. 1-11.

"And when he had gone a little farther thence, he saw James the son of Zebedee, and John his brother, who also were in the ship mending their nets. And straightway he called them: and they left their father Zebedee in the ship with the hired servants, and went after him."—MARK i. 19, 20.

THE MIRACULOUS DRAUGHT OF FISHES.

"Jesus said unto Simon, Fear not."—LUKE v. 10.

IT was left for Raphael to be the first painter to produce accurate and vivid representations of the incidents recorded in Holy Scripture, and it has remained for photography to give faithful impressions of his works. Raphael may be regarded as having photographed the Bible. We have, in his cartoons, almost the reproduction of the various scenes, just as we have in the photographs almost the reproduction of his pictures.

The photographs of the cartoons will be the means of attracting fresh attention to the best works of this artist, and as he laboured in them to expound the Word of God, "reading," in his way, "the book distinctly, and giving the sense," we propose entering into his labours; and we would invite those especially to join us who are heads of households, suggesting the use of the photographs, during some part of the Sunday leisure, as a thread on which may be strung some happy and holy words.

Bible pictures were our first means of grace. We have good reason to be grateful that we have had, from the earliest childhood, the Holy Scriptures pictorially presented to us. And nothing that we could say would, perhaps, be felt to be extravagance by those who, like ourselves, were trained up at a mother's knee on which was laid, week after week, a Sunday picture-book.

The publication of these photographs may serve to increase and educate the artistic tastes of the public; they may also, we hope, have another and higher tendency. The cartoons themselves are, we are persuaded, the work of a man who felt the power of the truth he delineated; "and by them he being dead yet speaketh." Those who have not been in a position enabling them to form a judgment, would, perhaps, be surprised as much at the character of his teaching, as at the number of his audience.

Raphael appears not only to have been diligent and successful in the pursuit of his profession, but also in the cultivation of that nobleness of character and genuineness of feeling, which made him a universal favourite with laymen and artists. His character was, doubtless, an essential element in his power to produce pictures which have won and kept the admiration of the world.

There is much common ground between painting and speaking. We all remember that it is laid down, by one of the first of the ancient writers of oratory, that a good speaker ought to be a good man. Goodness, as well as genius, seems to be as great a requisite for the artist as for the orator. Only the best of men can produce the best of pictures. This seems to be the rule. There must always be a harmony between a man and his works, if he attain to eminent success. A true picture, like a real book or an honest speech, is an exponent of its author. The man exhibits himself in his work. True works are wrought out of the abundance of the heart; it is this that gives them vitality. These true works differ as greatly as the hearts that produce them. There are many old pictures extant that are truly evil. They proceeded out of truly evil hearts. We may admire the genius and cleverness they manifest; but, as we gaze upon them, we cannot help thinking that only evil men could have produced such evil things.

Pictures should be good as well as true. A good picture must have a good subject. The picture may be correct in its drawing, natural in its colouring, and clever in its composition and treatment; but, except its story tells you some truth that appeals to your better nature, so that you are the better man for having seen, and understood, and felt, the artist's work, it had been better if the picture had never been painted.

The character of artists, as well as that of authors, may be argued from the choice of their subjects. And while we know that some have contradicted their teaching by their example, yet this discord has ever been more or less perceptible, and has always prevented " good success."

It is not only the nature of the subjects that Raphael chose for his pictures, but his method of their treatment, that leads you to suppose that his character was in keeping with his genius. He was free from the besetting sin of his profession. He was a stranger to envy and jealousy. There is a little picture which, in the absence of other evidence, may be allowed to give its testimony. When he was just of age, he painted for himself what has been called " The Dream of the Young Knight," in which he represents a youth, armed, who sees in a vision two female figures, one alluring him to pleasure, the other, with a book and a sword, urging him to study and to struggle. We have here, perhaps, an index of the conflict that was taking place within. He had, indeed, to fight the good fight under circumstances which render it very difficult for us to determine the issue. Let us hope that he had a victory given him by our Lord Jesus Christ.

The character of Raphael may be a matter of opinion; his power is a matter of fact. It is now four years since we began to work in the Cartoon Gallery, and, during that period, we have had ample opportunity of noticing the number, the class, and the conduct of the visitors. Considering the darkness of the room, and its distance from the entry of the palace, we have been surprised that there should be so many who, after their eyes had been distracted and satiated by the multitude of other pictures, were able to manifest the interest and feeling that we have seen and heard. Had the gallery been among the first rooms, and had it been lighted from the ceiling, the cartoons would have been oftener and better seen; but, even as things are, they are yet objects of great attraction, and sources of much power.

The cartoons are not popular. The great proportion of the company neglect them, as they do, alas! better things—for example, the Bible. As a rule, the visitors walk through the room without stopping, some not even looking on the walls as they pass on. There are, however, many happy exceptions. A coming party are often to be overheard talking together in the anteroom, pausing and uttering preparatory remarks, evidently conscious that there are not many such rooms as that which they are about to enter. These belong chiefly to the educated classes.

Hampton Court Palace is mostly frequented by the common people, and it is over them that the cartoons exercise the greatest power. We shall ever recollect our first Whitsuntide in the gallery. Forgetting the season, we had gone to our work as usual, on the Monday, and, the weather being very fine, we were soon reminded, by the swarming holiday folks, of the time of year. We had nearly turned back, but remembering that the bar across the room would secure us from interruption, we passed on, as quickly as we could, through the dense crowds. We anticipated that we should have the masses, after being pent up in rooms full of people and pictures, rushing through the gallery like a roaring tide, hasting to the outlet to the gardens. We were most gratefully disappointed. Many, but by no means a majority, walked through. The stream of the people stopped, those passing on forming only a narrow and hardly perceptible current. Crowds leant against the bar, and looked at the cartoons gladly. Some lingered as if they would never leave. Those who possessed scriptural knowledge sufficient to make them recognise the subjects of the pictures were evidently highly pleased to enlighten those who were at fault; and those who were unacquainted with the Bible narratives seemed determined to shew, by their remarks, that, though they had not read the Bible, they could read the cartoons.

You are not long, after you have become acquainted with the cartoons, before you have a kind of feeling, similar to that we have sometimes when we have been in company with a fresh acquaintance—you are reminded of a likeness, which at first was so indistinct that you could not recognise it. There are many points of

THE MIRACULOUS DRAUGHT OF FISHES.

similarity between the cartoons and the Bible. The quiet, grand way in which they speak to you; their strange power over all classes, and especially the common people; their perpetual freshness; the perfect subordination of the means to the end; the entire absence of all mannerism; the fact that, like the Bible, they belong to no time, person, or place—these things seem to produce within you sensations, somewhat resembling those we have after reading the Word of God.

On the before-mentioned day, we could not help feeling that, as in the Scriptures there are some passages hard to be understood, so there are perplexities in some parts of the cartoons, but that yet both tell their tales with such plainness and power, that the wayfaring men, though fools, cannot err therein.

The cartoons, like the Bible, were hidden for many years, and the world were only in possession of the tapestried interpretations. The history of their preservation has its wonders, as well as the memoirs of the Bible MSS. Both alike bear the traces of time, and both have suffered from interpolations. Of both there are many versions, and both, to be judged aright, must be studied in the original.

No engravings — although great genius was manifested by Dorigny, and great patience by Holloway—have ever given the full sense of the cartoons. The photographs are, after all, only a literal translation. To form a correct estimate of what the cartoons of Raphael are—to feel fully their power—they must be seen for themselves; and just as we find that the Bible reveals most of the word of God to us, when it is the first book in the day that we read, so the cartoons will only manifest themselves to those who have steadily refused to look at a single picture, as they passed through the various rooms, and have brought to the gallery a virgin eye.

Let us now look at the first cartoon. You not only at once recognise the scene depicted, but you can tell the exact moment which the painter has seized. Peter has presented his strange petition, "Depart from me; for I am a sinful man, O Lord." The strong tension of his mind yet keeps his body strung, and his arms and his hands in the attitude of prayer. Our Lord has begun His reply, "Simon, fear not; from henceforth thou shalt catch men."

The words of Peter must sound strangely in some ears. He had been graciously received by our Lord, when he was at the first brought to Him by his brother Andrew; and he must, we should have thought, have come to Jesus because he was a sinner. He has now made his sinfulness the ground of his prayer, that his Saviour should depart from him.

Some have thought that Peter did not mean what he said. These words have been supposed to be like those uttered afterwards on the Mount of Transfiguration, when "he wist not what to say, because he was sore afraid." There are others, however, who have some idea of the apostle's meaning—they are those who have been in similar circumstances, and have had the same feeling, if they have not said the same words. Our Lord at the time was "shewing forth His glory." God manifested Himself to Peter in the same way as He afterwards revealed Himself to Paul, and as He still appears to those who believe. Our sinful race has ever had, and will always have, the same experience.

Raphael has manifested a wisdom in the choice of this subject, and in the selection of this moment, which is only rivalled by the knowledge which he has displayed in its treatment. The painter lays the foundation of Peter's new life, in a perception that Jesus is the Son of God. The painter recognises the connexion between a call from God and godliness. Grasping this great truth, he still keeps his eye upon any details that may serve to complete its expression. For instance, amongst the figures in the carefully-executed background is a soldier. He is evidently the Capernaum centurion. The centurion had the same conviction of personal unworthiness as Peter, and on that ground, he was doubtless introduced by Raphael. There is nothing accidental in the rest

THE MIRACULOUS DRAUGHT OF FISHES. 9

of the landscape. It is all the production of one mighty in the Scriptures.

Our Lord is in Peter's boat; Andrew alone is their companion. Zebedee and his two sons have arrived, to rescue the draught of fishes from being lost. They tell you, by the strain on their muscles, that it has been a great catch. They stand stooping most awkwardly before you, overstrained, hauling at the miraculous multitude that are breaking their net. John and James are thinking only of the fishes. John only half turns his head; James is too much absorbed to do even that. Peter and Andrew suffer the fishes to escape over the boat-side. They discern the glory of the omnipotence of Christ. You can see the issues. Peter and Andrew will leave the fish and the nets and the boat, and follow Christ; James and John will return to the shore, with their father Zebedee and the fish, and mend their nets.

The figure of our Lord is an incarnation of Divinity. The form and the features, and even the drapery, distinguish Him as some one who is more than man. The contrast between our Lord and Zebedee is very striking. The one is sitting motionless, having awoke a deathless life in a soul, and seems, by a silent fiat, to have given the waves charge concerning the sinking boats. The other, with averted face, is more anxious for the boat than for the fish; with an utter unconsciousness of his nearness to the source of all power, he is lost in the exercise of his own weakness. The gulls in the air and the herons on the shore unite to tell their part of the story. They seem not only to anticipate a draught, but that the draught will be large, and that most of it will be left.

Those acquainted with the locality and the condition of the neighbourhood of the event, testify to the correctness of the outline of the shore. Any of us can see that the buildings are partly Oriental and partly Roman. The people who had heard our Lord speak are still to be seen; and others have arrived, bringing their sick and those possessed with devils.

The eye, in looking at this cartoon, is at once arrested by the figure of our Lord. We are often pained with some verbal, as well as with some pictorial representations of the Redeemer. It is a rare gift to "set Him forth evidently" before men. Raphael's success in painting may be envied by ministers in preaching. Here Christ is the first object of attention; and all the interest of the picture radiates from Him as the great centre.

Every one, of course, notices the smallness of the boats. Before adding to the countless and thoughtless criticisms that have been made upon this point, it may be well to recollect that we have here the work of a great man, and that even great men cannot perform impossibilities. It will be well to remember that whoever we are, and whatever may be our vocation, we are constantly obliged to choose between two evils. We cannot always do what we wish.

Raphael had to paint a series. The figures in all were to be of the same size. Had the boats been larger, these figures would have had to have been less. The figures being less, spectators might have imagined this subject to have been less important than the others. It was a choice between the figures and the boats, and the figures prevailed.

The extraordinary smallness of the boats may help us somewhat to understand the miraculous greatness of the draught.

We can now better understand the words of Peter, because we have better understood the circumstances in which they were uttered. The interest of the subject will never diminish. The scene here is repeated in the case of every Christian. Every one who follows Christ has been called by Him. The call has ever followed some personal revelation, some special manifestation of His power and glory; and as about Peter's call, and the manifestation of our Lord to him, there was some peculiarity, so there is always an individuality in His dealings with us all.

In this, as well as in other respects, "Jesus Christ is the same yesterday, to-day, and for ever;" and "as face answereth to face in a glass, so does the heart of man to man."

Before this event happened, Peter had been in contact with our

THE MIRACULOUS DRAUGHT OF FISHES.

Lord. He had called Him Master and Lord; but he had not forsaken all, and followed Him. Peter had returned to his home and his work. We shall be surprised at this fact, if we forget what we did ourselves, in the days of our first religious impressions, before God revealed His Son in us. Our Lord had come to seek and to save him. He, who once must needs go through Samaria to call the woman at Jacob's well, came to the Lake of Gennesaret to call Peter. The Great Fisher of men caught the fisherman with a miraculous draught of fishes.

Men are more influenced by works than words. Actions speak more loudly to them. Works are remembered when words are forgotten. All who would gain the attention of men, must act as well as talk. Our Lord came, not only speaking as none other man spake, but He came working as no other man wrought. His life appears to have been fuller of works than of words. He says Himself, "My Father worketh hitherto, and I work."

Our Lord sometimes invests the merest trifles with the greatest power. The photograph of this cartoon may be used by Him, to call some one to Him who reads this paper.

THE CARTOONS OF RAPHAEL.

No. II.

The Charge to Peter.

"After these things Jesus shewed himself again to the disciples at the sea of Tiberias; and on this wise shewed he himself. There were together Simon Peter, and Thomas called Didymus, and Nathanael of Cana in Galilee, and the sons of Zebedee, and two other of his disciples. Simon Peter saith unto them, I go a fishing. They say unto him, We also go with thee. They went forth, and entered into a ship immediately; and that night they caught nothing. But when the morning was now come, Jesus stood on the shore: but the disciples knew not that it was Jesus. Then Jesus saith unto them, Children, have ye any meat? They answered him, No. And he said unto them, Cast the net on the right side of the ship, and ye shall find. They cast therefore, and now they were not able to draw it for the multitude of fishes. Therefore that disciple whom Jesus loved saith unto Peter, It is the Lord. Now when Simon Peter heard that it was the Lord, he girt his fisher's coat unto him, (for he was naked,) and did cast himself into the sea. And the other disciples came in a little ship; (for they were not far from land, but as it were two hundred cubits,) dragging the net with fishes. As soon then as they were come to land, they saw a fire of coals there, and fish laid thereon, and bread. Jesus saith unto them, Bring of the fish which ye have now caught. Simon Peter went up, and drew the net to land full of great fishes, an hundred and fifty and three: and for all there were so many, yet was not the net broken. Jesus saith unto them, Come and dine. And none of the disciples durst ask him, Who art thou? knowing that it was the Lord. Jesus then cometh, and taketh bread, and giveth them, and fish likewise. This is now the third time that Jesus shewed himself to his disciples, after that he was risen from the dead. So when they had dined, Jesus saith to Simon Peter, Simon, son of Jonas, lovest thou me more than these? He saith unto him, Yea, Lord; thou knowest that I love thee. He saith unto him, Feed my lambs. He saith to him again the second time, Simon, son of Jonas, lovest thou me? He saith unto him, Yea, Lord; thou knowest that I love thee. He saith unto him, Feed my sheep. He saith unto him the third time, Simon, son of Jonas, lovest thou me? Peter was grieved because he said unto him the third time, Lovest thou me? And he said unto him, Lord, thou knowest all things; thou knowest that I love thee. Jesus saith unto him, Feed my sheep."—JOHN xxi. 1-17.

THE CHARGE TO PETER.

"He saith unto him, Feed my sheep."—JOHN xxi. 16.

IN looking at this cartoon, the eye is at once arrested by the keys in the hands of the apostle Peter. This circumstance has doubtless originated the mistake that is commonly made in reference to the subject of this picture. The keys are more conspicuous in the engravings than they are in the original, so that it is not surprising that those who are only acquainted with the work of Raphael through the medium of the press, should have fallen into the error, especially as many of the prints have received the title of "The Giving of the Keys." A superficial observer, seeing Peter kneeling with the keys in his hands, imagines that it was intended to portray the apostle as having just received spiritual authority, overlooking the plain evidence afforded by the body of our Lord, that the scene depicted must have occurred after the crucifixion.

The photograph is never likely thus to mislead a spectator. Here the keys are almost invisible. They can be discovered, but only by looking into the darkness in which they are obscured. The figure of our Lord is the first object that gains attention. The eye is carried forward by the lines of the outstretched arms, in the one direction, towards Peter, who is found upon his knees, humbling himself before the Saviour whom he has denied; in the other, toward the sheep which have, by artistic licence, been introduced. The subject of the picture is thus defined, and the exact moment clearly indicated. The penitent has just answered the question of our Redeemer, and he is receiving the commission, "Feed my sheep."

The peculiar weird-like effect of photography is in strange keeping with the scene here depicted. Raphael has evidently attempted to represent the body of our Lord after His resurrection, and he doubtless painted it in the light of the words of the evangelist John: "After these things Jesus *shewed* himself again to the disciples at the sea of Tiberias, and on this wise *shewed* he himself." You are reminded, as you gaze on this reflected figure, of the terms in which the various evangelists all speak of the manifestations of our Saviour, after He had risen from the dead. In the photograph, the body looks more like an appearance than a reality. You can now understand why Mary did not at first recognise its identity, and why, at this very time, when "Jesus stood on the shore, the disciples knew not that it was Jesus;" and that even after John had said to Peter, "It is the Lord," they would have liked to have asked the Saviour, if they had dared to do so, whether they were mistaken.

It is not often that an idea is improved by translation. An author is generally the best expositor of his own thoughts. It does, however, occur, though rarely, that a second mind, and sometimes another tongue, are required for the entire development of an original conception. There is, in this case, such an instance. The photograph, in two points, is superior to the cartoon. It is not only less ambiguous, but it is more impressive. Were Raphael to see this new version of his work, he would find that it had removed the possibility of mistaking the subject of his picture, and that it had developed from his cartoon, an effect that he himself could not produce.

The keys in the hands of the apostle have not only been the occasion of a diversity of opinion as to the purpose of the painting, but they have also originated discussions respecting his religion and his art. Connoisseurs have objected to the introduction of the symbols. They have questioned the artistic propriety of the keys and the sheep. They have argued that Raphael had no right, in painting such a picture, to turn figurative expressions into palpable objects. A sufficient answer to such affected Puritanism is found in the fact, that there were no other means of making the incident intelligible. The keys and the sheep form a great part of the whole story; they tell their tale as it could be told by nothing else, and they are in perfect keeping with the metaphorical teaching of our Lord.

The language of painting partakes of the weakness and poverty of other tongues; and thus artists are sometimes obliged, in common with other authors, to adopt foreign words.

Just as there are some who allow their sense of artistic propriety to interfere with their appreciation of the painter's work, so there are others who, in their criticism of his effort, suffer their Protestantism to get the better of their Christianity. There are those —the fact is stated on their solemn assurance—who are so shocked with the Papal badge, that they have decreed this picture to be utterly worthless to those who hold the Protestant faith.

The sectarian error is as manifest and as excusable as the artistic impropriety. Every artist is trammelled more or less by the patron for whom he works, and every religious man is influenced—sometimes very much against his will—by the party to which he belongs. The objections that have been raised by these professors of art, and these professors of religion, betray either a want of thought or a lack of charity. Raphael was a Romanist, and he had to decorate that portion of the Sistine chapel which was exclusively set apart for the use of the popes, and he very naturally introduced their heraldry.

Stumbling-blocks may serve as stepping-stones. The keys in the hands of the apostle had better remain where they are. They cannot be spared. They have misled others, but they may guide us. They have been abused, but "the abuse of anything is no argument against its use." The keys are neither ambiguous nor arbitrary. They are necessary and significant. They carry back the mind of the spectator to the time when our Lord entrusted the apostle with spiritual responsibility. Raphael teaches us, by the way in which he has treated the subject, the lesson which we all have great need to learn. The Peter before us is a sample of the race. Men are called by God and entrusted with a divine mission, but they forget their high vocation and fall away through unbelief, self-trust, and cowardice. Backsliders are not cast off and forgotten; but they are remembered, sought, and restored. The bruised reed is not broken—the smoking flax is not quenched.

The spiritual insight of the painter is as remarkable in this cartoon, as we found it to be in the last. Raphael evidently understood the origin of true religious conviction, or he could never have painted Peter, as God was manifesting Himself to him in the person of Jesus Christ. Raphael had made himself equally well acquainted with the Divine dealings toward those who have sinned against their conviction, or he could never have depicted Peter, remembering his iniquity before Him whose property it is ever to have mercy and to forgive.

The great end of our Lord's appearance to His disciples at the Sea of Tiberias, and especially of His conduct toward Peter, is to teach the long-suffering of the Divine mercy. The cartoon evidently sets forth the Good Shepherd, having laid down His life and taken it again, seeking His frightened and scattered flock. The apostles look like lost sheep. They are gathered together, but they are evidently not of one mind. They are not yet full of faith and full of the Holy Ghost.

The figure of our Lord is detached from those of His disciples. The drapery is so disposed as to leave His breast and His right arm bare. In a drawing, evidently made for this cartoon, we find Raphael had at first completely covered the body, so that the baring of the breast and the arm was the result of a second thought. In this way, the painter reminds us, that the incident took place subsequently to the crucifixion. The distance between Christ and His apostles, represents the difference of His communion with them after His resurrection from what it was before He suffered. As you look at our Lord, He seems to stand as if He were going away. As you look at the disciples, you see the spirit that they are of: they are yet

THE CHARGE TO PETER.

carnal; the mind that is in them is not the mind of Christ. One or two appear to be subdued and affectionate; but the others are displeased, jealous, and discontented. You feel that these men must receive power, and that the Holy Ghost must come upon them. You feel that it is expedient, that our Lord should go away to obtain for them that unspeakable gift.

The forty days which intervened between the resurrection and the ascension of our Redeemer, not only concluded our Lord's life upon earth, and His ministry in the body, but they were anticipatory to His spiritual reign in heaven. Our Lord gradually prepared His disciples for the final withdrawment of His earthly presence, manifesting Himself during these shadowy days in a manner that would tend to wean them from their dependence upon their senses. His visits were few and mysterious, and were confined to the first days of the week. The disciples seem to have understood the discipline, for we find that after His ascension they returned to Jerusalem with great joy, and continued with one accord in prayer and supplication, waiting for the promise of the Father, of which they had heard through Christ.

The records of these forty days are most precious to those of us who believe, and "they have been written for our learning, that we, through patience and comfort of these scriptures, might have hope." We know that "Jesus Christ is the same yesterday, and to-day, and for ever," and that He "is no respecter of persons." What our Lord was, when He shewed Himself at the Sea of Tiberias, He is now. The omnipotence He exerted on the behalf of His disciples, He is employing for us. We, like the disciples, labour in vain, and are not aware that our Lord is not very far from any one of us. We find all things working together for our good, and we are as dependent as they were, on the quicksightedness of some disciple whom Jesus loves, for the assurance, "It is the Lord." We are cold and hungry, and through the grace and providence of our Saviour we receive our fire and food. We eat and drink in His presence, sitting down to our meals, only half realising the wonders of His love; and we would, if we dared, ask for some manifestation of our Lord that He has not chosen to give.

It would appear, from the account that we have of what transpired on this, "the third time that Jesus shewed Himself to His disciples after that He was risen from the dead;" that whilst our Lord addressed Himself to the other disciples, the manifestation was intended especially for the one who had thrice denied Him. The miracle that preceded the conversation, would tend to confirm all of them in the conviction of the greatness of their future work, and it would give them a prophetic glance of their successful labour and abundant reward. The whole narrative, however, leads to the conclusion, that while the works and the words of our Lord were designed to influence the others, they were adapted particularly to affect the apostle Peter. The evangelist John, according to his custom, relates the miracle, not so much for its own sake, as for the conversation that followed it. Raphael, by placing the end of a boat in the corner of the picture, follows his example. The cartoon of "The Charge to Peter" contains the gist of the twenty-first chapter in the Gospel according to John.

The time has arrived when the recreant apostle is to be restored. Once and again our Lord had appeared to His disciples, but He has reserved the reinstatement of the backslider for this third manifestation of Himself. The Saviour seeks Peter where He had first called him; Peter is not only in the same place, but is engaged in the same employment. There are the same boats, the same companions, the same failure, and the same miracle.

The first object that is seen, as soon as the land is reached, is a fire of coals. It was at such a fire that Peter had stood and warmed himself, and denied his Lord.

The meal appears to have been eaten in silence. The company sit down in mysterious awe, wondering at our Lord, while they well know Him. No one hazards a word. At last, when they have dined, the stillness is broken by the Saviour. The threefold denial is recalled by the thrice-repeated question. Peter is addressed by the name he bore previously to his acknowledgment of Jesus the Son of God. Three opportunities are afforded him of contradicting his three denials. The apostle acknowledges the Divinity of our Lord, and appeals to His omniscience. He brings forth fruit meet for repentance. He no longer compares himself with others. He makes no promise. His answers are as full of godly sorrow as the questions of our Lord are full of love. Our Lord does not upbraid Peter, and Peter does not excuse himself. He was as a sheep going astray, but he is now returning to the Shepherd and Bishop of his soul.

This conversation has ever afforded instruction and comfort to the Church. This scripture is often searched by believers who have staggered through unbelief—by professors who have fallen through temptation. It is not our purpose to expound it; every word, especially if the passage be read in the original, will be found to be fraught with strong consolation. The distinctions made by our Lord in His three questions, (which are not apparent in our version,) are most affecting, and His three charges differ as greatly from each other as the three appeals of the apostle.

The photograph of "The Charge to Peter" has brought us to that fountain of mercy, where the apostle slaked the thirst of his guilt. We have, "on this wise," our Lord shewing Himself to *us*. The manifestation is for all, for "all we like sheep have gone astray;" and it may be the Saviour's purpose, thus to seek and to restore some one who has denied and deserted Him.

The voice of the Good Shepherd once heard is never forgotten. Those who have been in His fold, and gone in and out and found pasture, still remember and can still recognise the tone of His call, however far they may be in the wilderness, and however long it may be since they lost that sense of strangeness and terror, which overcame them when they first wandered. "He that hath ears to hear let him hear."

THE CARTOONS OF RAPHAEL.

No. III.

Peter and John Healing the Lame Man at the Beautiful Gate of the Temple.

"Now Peter and John went up together into the temple at the hour of prayer, being the ninth hour. And a certain man, lame from his mother's womb, was carried, whom they laid daily at the gate of the temple which is called Beautiful, to ask alms of them that entered into the temple; who, seeing Peter and John about to go into the temple, asked an alms. And Peter, fastening his eyes upon him with John, said, Look on us. And he gave heed unto them, expecting to receive something of them. Then Peter said, Silver and gold have I none; but such as I have give I thee: In the name of Jesus Christ of Nazareth rise up and walk. And he took him by the right hand, and lifted him up; and immediately his feet and ancle bones received strength. And he, leaping up, stood, and walked, and entered with them into the temple, walking, and leaping, and praising God. And all the people saw him walking and praising God: and they knew that it was he which sat for alms at the Beautiful gate of the temple: and they were filled with wonder and amazement at that which had happened unto him. And as the lame man which was healed held Peter and John, all the people ran together unto them in the porch that is called Solomon's, greatly wondering."—ACTS iii. 1-11.

PETER AND JOHN HEALING THE LAME MAN AT THE BEAUTIFUL GATE OF THE TEMPLE.

"Then Peter said, Silver and gold have I none; but such as I have give I thee: In the name of Jesus Christ of Nazareth rise up and walk."—ACTS iii. 6.

THE effect of this cartoon is both ornamental and picturesque. Raphael, in his treatment of the subject, has not only succeeded in representing this distinguishing feature of the place where the scene occurred, but he has also happily united two essentially different styles of beauty. There is here a wonderful combination of a pattern and a picture.

The painter, like other artists of his day, was an architect; and his success is to be mainly attributed to the wreathed columns, which he has introduced throughout the composition. These *twisted* pillars, (as they have been called,) have elicited the same captious remarks from those who have not known, or have forgotten, the work to be accomplished, as the keys in "The Charge to Peter," and the small boats in "The Miraculous Draught."

It has been already shewn that it is only just to the painter, in any judgment that is passed upon the cartoons, that their Papal origin and serial nature should be taken into consideration. It is equally necessary to remember their ultimate purpose. They were intended to serve as designs for tapestry. This circumstance explains many of those points which have excited observation. "In no other of Raphael's works are the compositions so simplified, or the masses kept so large and distinct. The colours are expressly selected, so as to profit by the splendour and variety of the hues of dyed wool and silk, with an intermixture of gold; and the drawing is so executed as to assist the mechanics who were to be employed in weaving these in tissue."

The use of a vehicle, which is only equal to express what is strictly ornamental, for the representation of the picturesque, is allowed to be a great mistake. This error is as palpable as the investiture of the apostle Peter with the Papal badge, or as the crowding three men into a boat that is barely sufficient to hold one. These points do not admit of a moment's debate. It would be impossible, by the exercise of any amount of ingenuity, to vindicate their correctness. They are untrue. Spectators are not requested either to defend or to ignore these inconsistencies. They are, however, asked to remember that they were unavoidable. We detain our readers —not that they may listen to any idle defence of Raphael, or to any impertinent apology for the methods in which he was obliged to treat his subjects—but rather that they may admire with us the triumph of his genius over the difficulties of his undertaking. These persecuted pillars, by their form, harmonise with the lines of the figures moving between them; by their position, seem to serve as frames for the various groups; and, by their elaborate detail, must have won golden opinions from the artisans at Arras.

The associations connected with the original situation of the tapestries, add to the interest and explain the intention of the cartoons, as much as the facts to which allusion has been made. Some knowledge of the place that Raphael was employed to decorate, is as necessary as some acquaintance with the conditions under which he had to labour. Another moment, then, good reader, as we trespass further upon your time, and beg you to turn aside and step into the building where our great painter might have been found, three hundred and fifty years ago, pondering over the commission he had received from Leo X.

This Sistine chapel received its name from Sixtus IV., who built it, for the special use of the popes, in 1483. It measures about one hundred and thirty-three feet in length, forty-three feet in width, and it is fifty-eight feet high. The white marble balustrade, that divides the area into unequal parts, is the boundary of the Presbyterium. Here the church ceremonies of the first Sunday in Advent and of the Holy Week are performed; and it is here that the scrutiny of the votes for the popedom is made, when the conclave meets in the Vatican.

The frescoes immediately below the windows, which extend entirely around the chapel, are the work of Perugino and others, who were employed by Sixtus IV. to represent the various Bible scenes. At the same time, the spaces underneath were painted in imitation of the embroidered hangings, which were used in the ancient Byzantine and Roman churches.

Nothing further was done till the accession of Julius II., the nephew of Sixtus IV. This prelate, remarkable for his vigour, enterprise, and taste, assembled around him the most distinguished artists of the day, and employed them in the prosecution of his ruling passion, the embellishment of the various courts and buildings which formed the palace of the successors of the Galilean fisherman. Under his direction, Michael Angelo covered the vaulted ceiling of the chapel with his frescoes. A certain plan having been already defined, the great painter took up the thread of the Bible history at its commencement—this had been carried on by Perugino; it was afterwards carried forward by Raphael, and it was at last completed by others.

Leo X., the successor of Julius, conceived the idea of placing real hangings, in the spaces of the walls of the Presbyterium that had been painted in imitation of tapestry. Raphael, who had been summoned to Rome by the aged Julius, and who was at work in another part of the Vatican, was employed by Leo to furnish designs for the Flemish weavers.

The cartoons are thus traced to their origin, and it may now be easily understood how the painter was determined in the choice of his subjects, by the place he had to decorate, and how his method of treatment was influenced, by the use which was to be made of his work.

The walls are divided, at regular intervals, into ten compartments, by painted pilasters adorned with arabesques. The tapestries were to hang in these spaces, and to be continued over the high altar. The Papal throne and the gallery of the choristers occupy part of two of the divisions, so that the tapestries in them would be much narrower than the rest. The number and size of the compartments determined the number and size of the cartoons. There are eleven divisions; and, originally, there were eleven cartoons—eight were large, one larger, and two were small.

The frescoes on the ceiling represent the creation of man—his fall, and the early history of the world. The advent of the Redeemer is depicted, more or less, beneath the windows. The tapestries told the mission, sufferings, and triumph of the Church. The whole series of pictorial decorations is closed by other works, in which we have the last judgment and the final blessedness of the saints.

The tapestries were hung in the following order:—" The Coronation of the Virgin" was placed over the high altar, the subject being chosen as a symbol of the triumph of Christianity. On the left, where it could not fail to catch the eye of "the head of the Church," was "The Miraculous Draught of Fishes." The conviction and the conversion of the apostle, who was regarded as the founder of the Papal dynasty, was selected as the subject to be immediately set before the pontiffs, as they seated themselves on the highest of earthly thrones. Then, following in order, "The Charge to Peter," "The Martyrdom of Stephen," occupying one of the small divisions; "The Healing of the Lame Man by Peter and John at the Beautiful Gate of the Temple," and "The Death of Ananias." The spaces on the right hand of the altar were devoted to the Apostle of the Gentiles. The subjects chosen for the tapestries were "The Conversion of Paul," "The Blinding of Elymas," "The Sacrifice at Lystra," "The Imprisonment at Philippi," and " Paul Preaching at Athens."

Raphael received for his cartoons the sum of £650, only a

hundredth part of the cost of the embroidery. The tapestries were completed in 1519; and the painter, before his death, (which happened shortly after,) had the satisfaction of finding, in the wonder and the applause of the whole city, that his difficult undertaking was considered to be a complete success.

The tapestries are now no longer hanging in the Presbyterium, the spaces on the walls appearing as they were originally painted. The woven relics are only exhibited once a year, and then they are hung in the great portico of St Peter, to grace the procession of the Corpus Christi. They are preserved, with a later series, in a corridor of the museum of the Vatican.

The peculiar richness of the effect, that is felt at the first glance at the cartoon of "The Beautiful Gate," not only reminds the spectator of the purpose to which it was to be applied, but it at once attracts his attention to the chief characteristic of the place, where the incident occurred which is here told.

The temple, in the time of the apostles, had nine gates, and there is a difficulty in fixing upon the one referred to by the sacred historian. All the gates, with one exception, were overlaid with silver and gold. It is possible, though by no means certain, that the gate, which consisted of Corinthian brass, and exceeded the rest in the magnificence of its design, was the place where "the cripple was laid daily, to ask alms of them that entered into the temple." The arbitrary value attached to the material of which it was composed, may be perhaps reckoned an additional argument in its favour. Raphael has taken the benefit of the doubt, and has shewn his wisdom in being governed, in his treatment of the architecture, by the idea of "beauty," which has special prominence in the Scripture record. The place, where the first recorded miracle of the Church was wrought, was subordinate to the miracle, just as the miracle itself was subordinate to its results.

It was impossible, and, as it happened, it was unnecessary, to represent "the Beautiful Gate." Raphael, therefore, designed these columns. Their spiral form bespeaks the grace of that entrance to the temple, which was daily haunted by that object of deformity, who is presently to receive a boon, without money and without price, which could not be purchased by silver or gold. The size, and perfect perpendicularity of the pillars, are standing proofs of the feebleness of the criticisms that have been made about their insecurity.

The miracle was not done in a corner. It was wrought in open day, and in the midst of a multitude. The scene occurred within the precincts of the temple at the hour of prayer, when it would be frequented by all sorts and conditions of people. Raphael, by making his architecture to consist mainly of twenty columns, standing four deep at regular intervals throughout the picture, has provided space in which the people can breathe and move; by placing the principal figures between the two centre pillars, has prevented their being lost in the crowd; and, by the double light, reminds us of the openness of the transaction and the sacredness of the place.

The eye, in the two other cartoons, is arrested by the figure of our Lord; here, though you do not see Him, you feel that you are in His presence. Your eye rests upon His apostles, who are evidently possessed with His Spirit. A great change has passed over Peter and John since we last saw them. They are evidently very different men to what they were. Their transformation is as remarkable, and as miraculous, as the act in which they are engaged. Both are inexplicable, except we believe that these men have received power, and that the Holy Ghost has come upon them.

Raphael was, without doubt, in possession of the greatest truths of Christianity. He has portrayed the origin of true conviction of sin, in "The Miraculous Draught of Fishes;" he has painted the fountain of mercy, the only hope and help of the backslider, in "The Charge to Peter;" and here, with equal definiteness, he bears his testimony to the dispensation of the Spirit. The choice of the subjects of these cartoons, and the method of their treatment, are clear proofs, that whatever might have been the real character of Raphael, he knew those truths that were able to make him wise to salvation. He must have perceived wherein the great strength of the Church lay, and he must have understood the laws of the kingdom of heaven, or he would never have selected this incident out of the multitude of the other acts of the apostles. It is not so much for its own sake that this miracle is recorded, as for the sake of its results. It led to the conversion of five thousand men, and to that first tribulation of the Church, which brought it in an agony of earnestness to that fervent effectual prayer which was answered by a second outpouring of the Holy Ghost, and a most marvellous deliverance from the selfishness of our nature.

Raphael seems to have anticipated, in the way in which he has represented the apostles healing the lame man, modern Biblical criticism. We are told to regard the book of "the Acts" as supplementary to the Gospels. In the Gospels we have "what Jesus began both to do and to teach, *until* the day in which he was taken up." In the Acts, we have the works and the words of our Lord, as He began to act and to speak through those who believed, *after* He had sat down on the right hand of God. As you look at this cartoon, you see that the act the apostles are performing is not their own; and it is this, as much as the miraculous nature of the work, that makes you conscious of the presence of Him who promised to be ever with them, and who is here evidently working in them to will and to do His good pleasure.

One of the reasons of the preciousness of this painter's works with spiritual men, is the strange power that he possessed of expressing the influence which Christianity has over the human countenance. He has exercised this ability in the cases of Peter and John with inimitable genius. The apostles look as if they were full of faith and full of the Holy Ghost. There is not the slightest trace of any self-sufficiency or pride. You might gather from their countenances that they do not imagine it is by their own power or holiness that they are making the man to walk. There is no anxiety. They are evidently fully persuaded in their own minds as to the result. A child, looking up into their faces, would feel at once that it might trust those benevolent, quiet, and strong men.

Raphael seems to have remembered and obeyed that law, which the greatest painter of character in words refers to in his lines—

> " A virtuous or a vicious spirit looks out
> In every limb and motion of the body."

The figures are full of expression from head to foot. Each limb tells its tale, contributing its part to the story of the conduct or the character of the person to whom it belongs. The impression produced by the countenance is confirmed by the concurrent testimony of the various members of the body.

The apostle Peter stands like a rock. His soul, "strong in the Lord and in the power of His might," seems to have lent its firmness to his whole frame. Those feet, that once staggered through unbelief, in their attempt to walk on the water, stand as if they had been set upon the marble pavement, in illustration of the quietness and confidence of a man who has faith in God.

The disciples, after the ascension of our Lord, often remembered His sayings. Their confessions and their quotations prove that the words of Christ " dwelt in them richly in all wisdom."

The promise which our Lord had made to Peter, that he should catch men, must, we imagine, have recurred to the recollection of the apostle when he preached in the streets of Jerusalem, with the thousands crying around him, " Men and brethren, what shall we do?" It may be that here he remembers the words uttered on the Mount of Olives: "Verily I say unto you, That whosoever shall say unto this mountain, Be thou removed, and be thou cast into the sea, and shall not doubt in his heart, but shall believe that those things which he saith shall come to pass, he shall have whatsoever he saith."

The time of the picture is that moment when Peter is saying, " In the name of Jesus Christ of Nazareth rise up and walk." Only Peter touches the cripple, and then but with one hand. He is not using his hand for the purpose of assisting the cripple in rising, but rather to form a link between one who evidently needs the help of Omnipotence, and another, who, by his uplifted hand, evidently implores the assistance of the unseen and Almighty God. The steadfast look of Peter and John, similar, perhaps, to that of Paul when he scanned the countenance of the cripple at Lystra, and perceived that he had faith to be healed, has passed away. The lame man, on whose face you read the record of forty years' helplessness, beggary, and pain, is under the influence of a wholly new class of feelings. His look of surprise tells you that he has never entertained the idea that he should ever walk. His coarse physiognomy—the result, perhaps, to a great degree, of the aggravating contempt of those who held opinions that were couched in the question put to our Lord, "Who did sin, this man or his parents, that he was born blind?"—his coarse physiognomy seems to reflect, for a moment, a brightness from those who are lifting up the light of their countenance upon him.

The repulsiveness that Raphael has succeeded in expressing in the faces and the figures of the crippled beggars, is as remarkable as the exquisite grace of the forms and attitudes of the women and the children whom he has placed beside them. It might be supposed, by those who are comparative strangers to sickness, disease, and deformity, that the painter had here exaggerated the effect of those evils. It may be said, that though this man was a cripple and a beggar, yet he had friends, and that their kindness would have had, by its constant and long exercise, some happy effect upon his character and appearance. A better acquaintance with the besetting sins of the class to which the man belonged, and a more thoughtful consideration of the Scripture record concerning him, will enable us to appreciate the truthfulness of the painter's conception. The man had friends, but they were either unable or unwilling to bear the burden of his support. To be carried twice a day, for years, to and from the temple at the hours of prayer, by persons who were able, but not inclined to render further assistance, must have been almost as insupportable as to lie there, and see the multitudes coming in and going out in the fulness of health and strength. Supposing, which may not be improbable, that those who waited upon the cripple were pitiful, though poor, still it would have been a hard trial for him to have added, and that daily and for years, to the difficulties of those who were weary and heavy-laden with the cares of this world.

The expression in the beggar's face might be attributed, though we hardly can conceive it, to the mental anguish of an independent spirit. The solution of the matter is, alas! very different. There is an unsightliness in all disease and deformity. There is, for the most part, a peculiar repulsiveness in the looks and appearance of those who have been afflicted with infirmities from their birth. This fact is too well known to those who are acquainted with the inmates of the hospitals and refuges which have been founded by Christian charity for their reception and care. In addition to this natural and, therefore, ordained connexion between repulsiveness and deformity, it is necessary to calculate, if it be possible, the force of those temptations of the diseased and deformed which make fearful havoc of what are called our natural good feelings. Only those who are the relatives, or those who are the nurses of the incurable, can form any correct estimate of the peevishness, selfishness, and tyranny of these miserable beings.* The expression of their countenances may be safely taken as an index of their character.

Raphael has fairly represented, in the cripple before us, the class to which the man belonged. The painter has, however, evidently wished us to understand that there are happy exceptions; he has, therefore, introduced a cripple resting upon a crutch, whose countenance is of a wholly different cast. You can see at once that he must have had some other support besides that wooden prop. His

---

* Miss Nightingale says, "Believe me, almost *any* sick person, who behaves decently well, exercises more self-control every moment of his day than you will ever know till you are sick yourself; if he can speak without being savage, and look without being unpleasant, he is exercising self-control."—*Notes on Nursing*, p. 35.

life has, indeed, been a walk through a valley of the shadow of death; but God has been with him, and His rod and His staff have comforted him. You are reminded, as you gaze upon that picture of resignation, of the words of one who went through great tribulation: "Unless Thy law had been my delights, I should then have perished in my affliction."

The words of Peter are evidently taking effect. They are mixed with faith by the man to whom they are addressed. The feet and ankle-bones, so palpably the seat of the lameness, will presently receive strength. "Everything is possible to him that believes, for with God nothing shall be impossible." We can see that faith in that Name which is above every name is making the man strong; the faith which is by Him is giving him perfect soundness. "Blessed is he that believeth; for there shall be a performance of those things that are told him from the Lord."

We may now turn and notice the surrounding figures, and we shall see how Raphael has provided for the relief of our feelings, after witnessing the miracle. The tension is gradually lessened. Our wonder and our gratitude are shared by many in the crowd. Those who are thronging the apostle John, and the soldier at the right-hand corner of the picture, evidently recognise the finger of God. Others appear to be in ignorance of what has happened, and some look on as if Peter and John had merely been giving money to the beggar, whom they had often noticed receiving alms. These persons are evidently those who are either just arriving at the gate, or those who have been into the temple and are passing out on their way home.

Raphael, by the treatment of his subjects, not only succeeds in fixing the attention of the spectator on the moment of the occurrence of the incident, but he enables him to recall the past and to anticipate the future. The connexion of events, and the passing nature of the scenes, are so represented as to excite sensations similar to those we experience in real life. After studying this cartoon, we find that we have been overhearing Peter and John discussing the question, whether they ought to go up to the temple to pray after the vail had been rent in twain, and they had given up their faith in its sacrifices; we have met the cripple as he was being carried, and have seen him laid against the column; we have witnessed the whole scene of the miracle. The spell continues upon us; and in the soldier we see the first of the five thousand who will hear and believe; in the look of the bigot, who stands by the adjoining pillar, (a monument of the power of prejudice,) we feel the darkening of the sky, and we anticipate the coming of the priest and the captain of the temple, and the imprisonment of Peter and John.

The accessory figures in this cartoon, like those in the others, have each its purpose. They are all necessary to the explanation of the painter's meaning. There are no redundant words in the sentence in which he utters his truth. The fulness and richness of the diction, in this instance, make the expositor's task almost endless. We must leave the other figures to our readers. Those who have learnt the pictorial alphabet will experience but little difficulty in perceiving why the painter has introduced the third cripple, and the mothers with their children. Those who are only beginning to read pictures, will find that they notice in the cartoons, the same points which attract their attention in common life, and that they will commence making their comments on the persons they see there, as if they had really met them. The young mother, for instance, who, with her attendant, is passing the soldier, evidently belongs to the higher class, and she is leaving the temple, after having presented, what appears to be, her first-born son. The mother, on the opposite side, whose boy is old enough to carry her sacrifice, is in humble circumstances; her offering is "the sacrifice of the poor;" the birds are pigeons, and from the state of their feathers, which are painted with great care in the original, you can see that they are young.

A trip to Hampton Court will shew the visitor, if he examines the tapestries in Wolsey's Hall, how utterly impossible it is to weave pictures. The Arras hangings were, indeed, far superior to

PETER AND JOHN HEALING THE LAME MAN.

these, but even those can only be regarded as elaborate failures and expensive mistakes. Persons seldom come to the Palace alone; should the visitor be accompanied by his daughters, we hope he will point out to them the necessity of confining their embroidery strictly to patterns.

The photograph of this cartoon will be specially appreciated after an examination of the present condition of the original. Photography has kindly and cleverly hidden the injuries of carelessness and the ravages of time. The picture itself will remind the spectator of some great ruin that he may have visited, which tasked his knowledge and his imagination to the utmost before he could produce an ideal restoration. The pleasure with which his eye may have rested upon some arch or pillar that has withstood the general destruction will be repeated as he stands before Raphael's work. Looking at the columns, and the crowd moving between them, he will feel, at first, that he is in the presence of universal decay, till he observes the faces of the mothers, and then, to his surprise and delight, he will find that the women have succeeded in preserving their good looks.

THE CARTOONS OF RAPHAEL.

No. IV.

The Death of Ananias.

" And when they had prayed, the place was shaken where they were assembled together; and they were all filled with the Holy Ghost, and they spake the word of God with boldness. And the multitude of them that believed were of one heart and of one soul: neither said any of them that ought of the things which he possessed was his own; but they had all things common. And with great power gave the apostles witness of the resurrection of the Lord Jesus: and great grace was upon them all. Neither was there any among them that lacked: for as many as were possessors of lands or houses sold them, and brought the prices of the things that were sold, and laid them down at the apostles' feet: and distribution was made unto every man according as he had need. And Joses, who by the apostles was surnamed Barnabas, (which is, being interpreted, The son of consolation,) a Levite, and of the country of Cyprus, having land, sold it, and brought the money, and laid it at the apostles' feet. But a certain man named Ananias, with Sapphira his wife, sold a possession, and kept back part of the price, his wife also being privy to it, and brought a certain part, and laid it at the apostles' feet. But Peter said, Ananias, why hath Satan filled thine heart to lie to the Holy Ghost, and to keep back part of the price of the land? Whiles it remained, was it not thine own? and after it was sold, was it not in thine own power? why hast thou conceived this thing in thine heart? thou hast not lied unto men, but unto God. And Ananias, hearing these words, fell down, and gave up the ghost: and great fear came on all them that heard these things. And the young men arose, wound him up, and carried him out, and buried him. And it was about the space of three hours after, when his wife, not knowing what was done, came in. And Peter answered unto her, Tell me whether ye sold the land for so much? And she said, Yea, for so much. Then Peter said unto her, How is it that ye have agreed together to tempt the Spirit of the Lord? behold, the feet of them which have buried thy husband are at the door, and shall carry thee out. Then fell she down straightway at his feet, and yielded up the ghost: and the young men came in, and found her dead, and, carrying her forth, buried her by her husband. And great fear came upon all the church, and upon as many as heard these things."
—Acts iv. 31-37, v. 1-11.

THE DEATH OF ANANIAS.

"And Ananias, hearing these words, fell down."—ACTS v. 5.

THE cartoon of "The Death of Ananias" has been placed over the door of the Gallery at Hampton Court, and is the least noticed of the whole series. This is to be attributed partly to its position. Very few visitors, by the time they have reached this point in their stroll through the state apartments, have the energy left to turn round; they may glance, in passing, at the other cartoons, (although they have been placed above the line of the eye,) but they do not care to trouble themselves to turn round and look up at this one, which hangs over their heads. Even when the picture happens to be noticed, it is not often seen; and when it is seen, it is not liked. Lost in darkness most of the year, it only becomes visible in the summer; and then when, on a bright day, it may be discovered by some indefatigable sight-seer, its subject is found to be repulsive. "The Death of Ananias" is not a subject that can be expected to commend itself to a party of pleasure. Some one of those whose attention may have been arrested, may be found gazing at it with that look which bespeaks the frequenter of "The Chamber of Horrors;" but the rest will turn away with an abruptness which manifests their settled determination that nothing, if they can prevent it, shall spoil their holiday.

The spectator, especially if he belongs to the school which refuses to acknowledge the realities of life, should remember the mission of Raphael, or he may too readily condemn the taste of the artist in choosing to depict this terrible scene. This cartoon was not painted to hang among the pictures at a place of amusement, but it was originally designed for the Sistine Chapel at Rome. It was not intended to disturb those who were seeking relaxation in a day's pleasure; but it was meant to meet the eye of those who professed to have renounced even the most innocent enjoyments of this world. The choice of the subject, instead of furnishing any ground for disputing the taste of Raphael, should be regarded as a proof of his courage. He was not afraid to place before those who were making the greatest pretensions in Christendom the fearful doom of the first hypocrite in the Christian Church.

The passage that contains the narrative of this fact is found generally to be as repulsive as its pictorial representation. Very few readers of the Bible search the scripture that records the death of Ananias. If it be read through at all, it is, for the most part, so hastily passed over, that the popular errors that prevail concerning the occurrence are not discovered. There is also a very general indisposition to believe in the severity as well as the goodness of God, and thus it is that this event is regarded with so much prejudice and perplexity.

The incorrectness of some of the divisions of the Bible into chapters and verses has often led to a misconception of revealed truth. Very frequently, as in the present case, the text is so mutilated, that the cursory reader receives only a partial, and therefore an erroneous, impression of the Divine record. "The Death of Ananias" has become one of "those things which are hard to be understood, which they that are unlearned and unstable wrest, as they do also the other scriptures, unto their own destruction."

We do not imagine that our readers are strolling through this world, making their whole life a day of pleasure, having determined to shut their ears to truths, and to turn away their eyes from facts, which might lead them to examine themselves, whether they be in the faith. Had they been merely pleasure-seekers, we should long ere this have become tired of each other. If, however, we had met

THE DEATH OF ANANIAS.

any of them in the Cartoon Gallery, as they were strengthening themselves by a day of relaxation, we should not have drawn their attention to this cartoon, and most assuredly, we should not have forced upon them any untimely exposition of its fearful subject. We suppose our readers to be at home, and that, looking at the photographs, they read these papers in very much the same spirit as that in which they are written. We will not do them the injustice to fancy that it is the opinion of any of them that Ananias was struck dead by Peter, or that Sapphira was led to criminate herself by the questioning of the apostle. The only light in which a picture can be fairly seen is that light in which it was painted; and we write under the conviction that our readers occupy the same position as ourselves—that they believe in the Divine severity as well as the Divine goodness—that they have discovered hypocrisy to be the sin that most easily besets us as religious men—and that they regard hypocrisy as the lie direct to God.

If the text of Raphael's copy of the Scriptures had been separated in the same manner as that in our own version, then the painter deserves credit for a discernment in which even many a Bible expositor has been deficient. He has taken the unbroken narrative, and, working in the light of the context, he has represented the scene in a manner which will commend itself to those who read the Bible in paragraphs rather than in chapters.

The painter had found that it was impossible to reproduce the architecture of the Beautiful gate of the temple, and that its delineation was unnecessary in setting forth the story of the miracle on the lame man. He, however, saw that a representation of the upper room in an Eastern house was absolutely requisite in any picture of "The Death of Ananias," which would unfold the mystery of his iniquity and the justice of his doom. We have, therefore, in this cartoon, one of those apartments which had been constructed for the use of the Jews who came up to Jerusalem at the various feasts. The railed platform (evidently of late erection) has been introduced by the apostles for the purpose of facilitating the reception and the distribution of the new-born charity of the Church. The commonness of the material of which it is composed, the manifest cheapness of the whole structure, with the meagre curtain which hangs at the back, all shew that the greatest economy has been observed. On the right hand, those enter who are giving up their property; on the left hand, "distribution is made to every man according as he has need." The double-minded man mingles with these single-hearted people. He is accompanied by Barnabas, who, with his wife, or some near relative or friend, are represented to have been kneeling and laying their whole fortune at the feet of the apostles.

The enormity of a sin is dependent not only upon the character and the circumstances of a criminal, but also upon the place where it is committed. If, therefore, as it is probable, Ananias was in the very room where there had been, only very lately, sensible proofs of the Divine presence; if this was the place where the ten-days' prayer-meeting had been held, and where the apostles were filled with the Holy Ghost; and if, above all, this was the large upper room so strangely marked out by our Lord as the place where He would eat the Passover with His disciples in the night in which He was betrayed; then, "surely, it was none other than the House of God and the Gate of Heaven;" and the guilt of Ananias becomes more apparent, and the awfulness of his doom less astounding.

It is for us, however, to remember, that we are utterly unable to form any correct estimate of the iniquity of deceit. We do not understand the sin, and therefore we cannot understand the sentence of Ananias. There are times and seasons when the darkness in which this event is for the most part obscured is somewhat dissipated, just as there are days when the cartoon becomes visible, but even then we only see through a glass darkly. As long as we are in the twilight of this world, sin and death will remain mysteries to us. We must wait till we stand in the light in which there is no darkness at all, before we can comprehend either the severity or the goodness of God. "Now we know in part, but then we shall know even as we are known."

THE DEATH OF ANANIAS.

Whatever may be the popular opinion, we read that "Our God is a consuming fire." The death of Ananias, the death that is common to all men, the death of our Lord and Saviour Jesus Christ, are all manifestations of the holiness of God, His hatred of iniquity, and His purpose to put away sin. Light is thrown upon the sin of the world by the death of our Lord,—upon the sin of disobedience by the death that passes upon all men,—upon the sin of hypocrisy by the death of Ananias.

The judgments of God are past finding out—"His way is in the sea, and His path in the great waters, and His footsteps are not known." It is worse than idleness to attempt to be wise above what is written, in order to justify the ways of God to men. No complete explanation can be given of the death of Ananias, or of the death of any man, much less of the atoning death of our Redeemer. "None can by searching find out God, none can find out the Almighty unto perfection." "The secret things belong unto the Lord our God; but those things which are revealed belong unto us and to our children for ever, that we may do all the words of His law."

The subject of this picture is as difficult to expound as it must have been to paint; and any expositor may sit with advantage at the feet of Raphael, and learn the only possible way in which it may be successfully treated. The great artist had evidently no other design than that of representing the fact as he found it set down in the Sacred Record; and he felt that if he followed the Scripture story, a similar effect would be produced by his picture as that which resulted from the scene it delineates. Raphael painted from revelation as he painted from nature. It is in this that his great strength lies, and it is this which makes the cartoons so precious to those who wish to realise the scenes they delineate, and to learn the lessons they were intended to teach.

Finding that the narrative had been recorded for the perpetual admonition of the Church against hypocrisy, forgetting the conventional laws of taste, Raphael seems to have been wholly swayed, in the composition and treatment of this cartoon, by a desire to echo the Divine Warning. This purpose not only led him to choose this subject, but it governed him also in the selection of the time of the picture.

The Apostle Peter has just spoken, and Ananias has fallen to the ground. Barnabas and his companion start back with horror, finding that they have been holding communion with one who was of "the fellowship of Satan." The body of the hypocrite is writhing in convulsions, and in another moment it will be a corpse. The catastrophe is so sudden, that it is seen and known only by those who happen to be near at the time. Two Christians who have come to present their offerings are the closest figures; neither of them, however, offer to support the dying man, who rests for a moment on his left wrist. The apostles leave him to perish in his iniquity, looking on, as if they had been suddenly endued with those feelings which will be given to the redeemed in the last and great day of account. Ananias is dying without mercy, but one person seems to suppose that there is a shadow of hope, and he only half stoops to point the insensible man to the Apostle James, who, by his uplifted hand, reminds the disciple that the judgment has been inflicted by One against whom there is no appeal.

The age and character of Ananias are told with great clearness. He is represented as having been in middle life, and of a coarse appearance. Overacting his part, he had stripped himself of his upper garment, and in that, may be, he is wound up, and hurried to his grave. Perhaps his money was buried with him.

Turning away from this awful revelation of the severity of God, we come directly into contact with that manifestation of His goodness, which He was displaying in the conduct of those who really believed. The Apostle John, and another disciple, are attending to the claims made upon the bounty of the Church; and the distribution of the charity is represented to have been undisturbed at the first part of the scene. The painter thus expresses the unexpectedness of the catastrophe, and at the same time alleviates the feeling

THE DEATH OF ANANIAS.

of the spectator. There is apparently (and this is, doubtless, the cause of the abstraction of the distributors) some difficulty raised by a claimant, who is evidently, from the expression of his countenance, dissatisfied with the amount which he is receiving. Raphael is thus suggesting, as in his introduction of Sapphira on the opposite side, the future. We have in the beggarly face of the man, who is discontented with the portion allotted to him, the hint of the murmuring of the Grecians against the Hebrews, because their widows were neglected in the daily ministrations. Our knowledge of human nature enables us easily to understand, that no distribution of charitable funds, although made by apostolic hands, would give universal satisfaction.

The scripture recording this awful judgment was written for our admonition who profess and call ourselves Christians; and those amongst us will do well to take heed to it, who have linked the destiny of another with our own. A profession of religion was the ruin of Ananias. That which might have been a savour of life unto life, became a savour of death unto death. The means of grace issued in damnation. Carried by the pressure of the multitude into the holy of holies, he was detected, denounced, and doomed. "He fell down, and gave up the ghost;" for he was where only the just can live, and where a foothold can only be maintained by faith. Had Ananias been content to keep the whole of his property, and to make the best of this world, he would, in all probability, have lived on, and died the death that is common to all men. Had he been unmarried, he would have escaped the fearful force of the temptation that besets the closest relationship into which we are brought in this life; the idea of the possibility of making the best of both worlds might have occurred to him, and he might have made some other attempt to serve God and Mammon; the words of the apostle, however, lead to the supposition that this iniquity was the result of the united influence of the man and the wife over each other, and that, without the strength of this union, their hearts would not have been fully set to do this evil. Which of the unhappy pair was first in the transgression, does not appear; no time is allowed the man who introduced hypocrisy into the second Eden, to lay the blame upon his wife. The woman betrays her reprobate mind by her answer to Peter; had she been an unwilling accomplice, she would have seized with gratitude the opportunity for confession which was afforded her by the question of the apostle. Both of them, however, appear to have gone too far to return. Neither had the disposition to repent; making shipwreck of faith and a good conscience, they had become alike hardened through the deceitfulness of sin. They had united themselves in their hypocrisy, and they were not divided in their death.

Further light is thrown upon the *Sin* of Ananias by the remembrance of the contest, that has lasted for six thousand years in this world, between the God of truth and the father of lies;—that this man lived at the commencement of the final conflict, which is to end in the destruction of the works of the devil, and the restoration of the redeemed to the uprightness in which the race was at first created;—and above all, that Ananias had been made partaker of the Holy Ghost, that he had been enlightened, and tasted of the heavenly gift, but that, quenching the Spirit, he held the truth in unrighteousness. It was at such a time, and in such a condition, that he came as the people of God came, and knelt where they did; and while they were yielding up themselves and all they had, he presented to the God of truth the offering of a lie.

Further light is thrown upon the *Death* of Ananias when we remember that the severity as well as the goodness of God had been just manifested in a way in which it had never been before displayed. Ananias lived when God was manifest in the flesh. Neither the Divine justice nor the Divine mercy had been ever seen, or ever known, till the only-begotten Son, who is in the bosom of the Father, declared them. A few weeks before this awful visitation, our Lord had come to the Church, to whom less was given, and convicted, warned, and denounced the hypocrites that He found there; the Church of whom more was required, would be

THE DEATH OF ANANIAS.

forewarned, by the loudness and nearness of the thunder, of the danger that hung over them, if it did not take heed and beware of the leaven of the Pharisees.

The facts of Scripture, like the events of Providence, should be studied in their connexion. In this way, many narratives and many circumstances become less perplexing, though not less mysterious. The popular surprise and horror, which are occasioned by reading the first verses in the fifth chapter of the Book of the Acts, (and which utterly prevent the wholesome fear which the event was intended to produce,) will never be felt by those who are accustomed to search, remember, and compare the Scriptures. There are passages, both in revelation and in providence, that should never be contemplated alone. The reading of the record of the doom of the first hypocrite in the Christian Church should be ever preceded, or followed, by the study of the 23d chapter in the Gospel according to Matthew.

THE CARTOONS OF RAPHAEL.

No. V.

The Conversion of Sergius Paulus.

"And Barnabas and Saul returned from Jerusalem, when they had fulfilled their ministry, and took with them John, whose surname was Mark. Now there were in the church that was at Antioch certain prophets and teachers; as Barnabas, and Simeon that was called Niger, and Lucius of Cyrene, and Manaen, which had been brought up with Herod the tetrarch, and Saul. As they ministered to the Lord, and fasted, the Holy Ghost said, Separate me Barnabas and Saul for the work whereunto I have called them. And when they had fasted and prayed, and laid their hands on them, they sent them away. So they, being sent forth by the Holy Ghost, departed unto Seleucia; and from thence they sailed to Cyprus. And when they were at Salamis, they preached the word of God in the synagogues of the Jews: and they had also John to their minister. And when they had gone through the isle unto Paphos, they found a certain sorcerer, a false prophet, a Jew, whose name was Bar-jesus: which was with the deputy of the country, Sergius Paulus, a prudent man; who called for Barnabas and Saul, and desired to hear the word of God. But Elymas the sorcerer (for so is his name by interpretation) withstood them, seeking to turn away the deputy from the faith. Then Saul, (who also is called Paul,) filled with the Holy Ghost, set his eyes on him, and said, O full of all subtilty and all mischief, thou child of the devil, thou enemy of all righteousness, wilt thou not cease to pervert the right ways of the Lord? And now, behold, the hand of the Lord is upon thee, and thou shalt be blind, not seeing the sun for a season. And immediately there fell on him a mist and a darkness; and he went about seeking some to lead him by the hand. Then the deputy, when he saw what was done, believed, being astonished at the doctrine of the Lord."—ACTS xii. 25, xiii. 1-12.

THE CONVERSION OF SERGIUS PAULUS.

"Then the deputy, when he saw what was done, believed, being astonished at the doctrine of the Lord."—ACTS xiii. 12.

BY this time, our readers must be finding themselves somewhat at home amongst the cartoons,—able, in some measure, to understand the secret of Raphael's power over them, and ready to anticipate the profit and the pleasure which are still in reserve. They will remember that the three cartoons which have yet to be studied, form part of the series of five, in which the painter represented the leading events in the life of Paul, and that the first and the fourth are lost.

Some twelve years transpired between the Death of Ananias and the Conversion of Sergius Paulus. It may be well just to glance at the connexion of these events. The dissatisfaction that was manifested, in the last cartoon, amongst some who were receiving alms, led to the election of special officers for dispensing the charity of the Church. One of these deacons, "Stephen, a man full of faith and the Holy Ghost," made himself obnoxious to the Sanhedrim, and met with a violent death at the hands of a Jerusalem mob. His murder was followed by the persecution of the Church, and the conversion of Saul. The apostles remained mostly at Jerusalem. The scattered believers went everywhere, even as far as Cyprus, preaching the word, but "preaching the word to none but unto the Jews only."

Saul appears to have spent in Arabia the first three years after his conversion, and there he doubtless received that revelation of "*his*" gospel, of which he afterwards makes such frequent mention in his letters. Returning to Damascus, he is driven thence by the hostility of the Jews; and going up to Jerusalem, where (by the mediation of Barnabas) he obtains an acknowledgment from the apostles of his Christianity, he is again persecuted and obliged to flee for his life. Saul had been spending several years at Tarsus, when he is at last sought out by Barnabas, who had been commissioned by the Church at Jerusalem to visit Antioch. In this city, where Gentiles were received into Christian fellowship with Jews, Paul and Barnabas " assembled themselves a whole year with the church, and taught much people." It was at this place, and at this time, that " the disciples were first called Christians;"—at the place where " the middle wall of partition was first broken down"—at the time when, moved by the Holy Ghost, the Church began to see that " Jesus Christ was the propitiation not for their sins only, but also for the sins of the whole world."

Raphael, with his accustomed spiritual insight, has selected this era in the history of the Church for illustration; and we have, standing before us in this cartoon, the man who first began to go throughout the whole world, and to preach the gospel to every creature. The first cartoon in the series which was devoted to the history of the life of Paul, depicted his conversion and his call. That has been lost; this, which is the second, represents him at the commencement of his first missionary journey.

The ordinary title of this cartoon would lead the spectator to suppose that its subject was " The Blinding of Elymas," rather than that which has been placed at the head of this paper. We are not alone, happily, in an opinion that this picture was painted with the same purpose as that for which the scripture was written in which we have the record of the event it describes. A careful reader of the 13th chapter of the Acts will gather from the narrative that the sacred historian is giving an account of "The Conversion of Sergius Paulus." "The Blinding of Elymas" is referred to, but only as a subsidiary fact. " The Conversion of Sergius Paulus" is

THE CONVERSION OF SERGIUS PAULUS.

the subject of the Bible paragraph, and the attentive spectator will find it to be the subject of the cartoon.

At first sight there appear to be three principal figures—the apostle, the proconsul, and the sorcerer. The eye, instinctively following the direction in which the attention of the whole company is turned, rests for a time upon Elymas, who is crouching under the sudden judgment of blindness; unsatisfied, it is led away by the index finger, which is pointing over the sorcerer's head, towards Paul; dwelling, at last, on the central figure, (perhaps because it is the only one that is seated,) the spectator begins to feel that he must study Sergius Paulus, if he would discover the event that is taking place. He studies in vain, till, a little under the line of the eye, he discovers the printed directions of the artist, and reading them, he understands, at last, the scene that is passing before him. We approach this picture much in the same way as we are sometimes drawn to a crowd; we look on, and though we have a good view of the passing transaction, we are utterly unable to understand what is taking place, till we are distinctly told by some bystander.

It would seem that the device was beneath the genius of the painter, and that by a different method of treatment, he might have obviated the humbling necessity of a verbal explanation. Raphael appears to have been free from the anxieties that are ever disturbing inferior men. He had no petty ambition to appear to be omnipotent. He knew, and was not afraid to acknowledge, the limit of his art. He, of course, lays himself open to the imputation of weakness, but he does so with the same unconcern as, in taking his figure of Paul from Masaccio, he exposes himself to the charge of plagiarism. Raphael was so well known to be rich, that he could afford to borrow, and with his well-earned reputation for strength, he might be careless about any appearance of weakness.

The inscription, which occupies so prominent a place, was of course intended to attract the attention of every spectator, and we have but to read it to admire the humility and the wisdom of the painter. Holloway, in order, perhaps, to preserve the title of his engraving, "Elymas the Sorcerer struck with Blindness," has, very consistently, omitted Raphael's explanation. The photograph, with its incorruptible fidelity and unreasoning wisdom, has given every word.

There is now no question about the principal figure, or the subject of the cartoon. The scene before us is no more "The Blinding of Elymas" than it is "The first Appearance of Paul as the Apostle of the Gentiles." Both those events were subsidiary. The apostle and the sorcerer are represented in the cartoon as they are brought before us in the Scripture narrative, as secondary figures. The conversion of the proconsul is declared by the sacred writer to be the issue of the conflict between Elymas and Paul. The cartoon echoes the words in which the historian closes his account, "Then the deputy, when he saw what was done, believed, being astonished at the doctrine of the Lord."

The great and ineffable change that was passing over Sergius Paulus was beyond the power of Raphael to paint. He has, nevertheless, done what he could. We have before us the persons who were present at the time, and we can witness the event that was the means of his turning to the faith.

The artist has adopted the same circular arrangement of the various figures as in the last cartoon, elevating those that are more distant, so that every one can see and be seen. But while this point of similarity may be observed, we cannot help noticing the striking difference between the two companies, and the two places where they are gathered together. Barnabas, who is half-hidden between two of the pillars of the Roman court, and who ever occupies a subordinate position in this novel mission to the Gentiles;—Mark, who peers over the shoulder of one of the lictors, and looks as if he were half inclined to run away from Paphos, as he did presently from Perga;—seem to remind us, that a step has been taken, which was completely at variance with the doctrine and the practice of the Church at Jerusalem.

As we look at Paul, "called of God and separated by the Holy

Ghost to bear the name of Christ before the Gentiles and kings," we feel that he has commenced a career which will estrange him from his fellow-believers, and which will issue in his persecution, imprisonment, and death.

Paul has been travelling across the island of Cyprus, (doubtless walking, "carrying his baggage;") and he has no sooner arrived at the seat of government, than he is sent for by "one in authority," whose heart the Lord must have opened, for "he desires to hear the word of God." Personal defects are frequently forgotten in times of excitement. We are unconscious of any bodily infirmity in that draped figure, as we gaze upon it, standing before us with its outstretched arm, as one having convictions and an opportunity to express them. The apostle himself, for the moment, has evidently lost sight of "his thorn in the flesh."

Turning to the opposite corner, we find Bar-jesus, one of those wandering Jews who infested the Roman empire, trading upon the universal scepticism and superstition of the times. The false prophet, evidently one who has not been carried away by his own delusions, seems to be accompanied by his wife and a disciple. He feels that, as Paul reasons of righteousness, the proconsul is evidently listening, and is disposed to believe. The hope of his gains is going, and, "full of all subtilty and mischief," he withstands the apostle, "seeking to turn away the deputy from the faith."

Sergius Paulus, supported on the one hand by lictors bearing the fasces, and on the other by some superior officer, has been seated listening first to Paul, and then to the attempt made by the sorcerer to regain his loosened grasp, when a mist and a darkness from the Divine hand silences with blindness "the enemy of all righteousness, who is perverting the right ways of the Lord." The judgment upon Elymas is the means of the conversion of the proconsul. While the mist has been changing into a darkness over Elymas, a light has shone into the heart of the deputy. His face, as yet, betrays no sign of his having escaped from the thraldom of sin and Satan. He still retains his seat. He appears as if he would have risen, but is kept from doing so, not from the habit of official etiquette, (for the time is too serious for such a recollection,) but from horror, lest he come into contact with the detected deceiver, as he gropes about "seeking some to lead him by the hand."

There are difficulties connected with this event, as there are with most others. Many objections may be urged by those who are not "slow to speak," against the judgments of God. Those who are inclined, can stay and listen to the angry clamour of the woman, who points to Paul as if he had been the author of the calamity, and who seems to forget that the blindness was to be only "for a season." Let us hope that those who hear what this foolish woman has to say, will receive her vociferations in the same manner as that company of quiet, thoughtful men, whom she is endeavouring to inflame with her passion. If we be ever moved, by some sudden and severe stroke, to murmur against God, let us pray that there may be as near to us as there is to this woman, some one who shall point out to us the goodness that is ever to be seen in the severity of God.

A Christian will be reminded by this cartoon of what may have transpired at his own conversion, and of a fact that he may have verified as he has sought the conversion of others. He may remember, that when Divine grace began to work upon his mind, leading him to "desire to hear the word of God," there was, on the one hand, some one in whom the Spirit of the Lord was—it might have been a mother, a minister, a friend, or a teacher—who sought to turn him from the error of his way, and to save his soul from death. In direct antagonism to this heavenly agency, there was, on the other hand, some companion who had gained power over him, and who was using that power to prevent his salvation. The same attempt is ever repeated; and this record of the conversion of Sergius Paulus seems to have been written for the special admonition of those who are being thus hindered in their own salvation, or in the salvation of others, "that they, through patience and comfort of this scripture, might have hope." The Son of God has been, and ever will be, manifested in the destruction of the works of the devil.

As soon as we are able to disengage the attention which Raphael has concentrated upon this scene, we begin to notice some of those details in the design and execution of the cartoon, which, almost as much as the unity of its effect, betray the hand of a master. The disciple of the sorcerer, deaf to the clamour of his master's wife, looks into the blinded face of the baffled man, and tells us as he does so, not only that it is too true that Elymas cannot see, but that he feels the judgment to be as just as he finds it to have been effectual. The same knowledge of the connexion that exists between the countenance and the character that is displayed in the representations of Elymas and his follower, is shewn again in the low, brutal expression in the faces of the lictors. The hands and feet of the various figures are marvellous instances of masterly drawing.

There is, however, no time for us to lose. Following the dictate of an instinct which teaches us the wish of the majority of our readers, who have been arrested, like ourselves, with the figure of Paul, we turn back to gaze upon it. This ideal portrait is by no means popular. Most regard it with feelings of surprise and disappointment. Every one, of course, admires the idea, but many question its truth. A few of the spectators, who belong to the growing school of muscular Christianity, will be gratified to find that the apostle, who has had most influence over them, is so represented by Raphael, that they may very fairly quote both the painter and his subject in favour of their theory. The rest regard it as a mistake and an offence.

It may be necessary for some who would hastily condemn this embodiment of the apostle as unnatural, to remember that often, in real life, we are mortified, and even shocked, when we have been for the first time introduced to some one whose image has long lived in our fancy; that we are all portrait-painters, and exposed to the besetting sin of the profession; that we vary in taste and talent, and necessarily produce our pictures in such a way as to make it highly probable that our likenesses of a person will differ as greatly from each other as they often do from the original.

Much of the surprise which this representation creates may be attributed to the fact that, for the most part, the ideal portraits of the apostle consist merely of a few confused lines, mingled with some doubtful traditionary touches; whereas, here, we have a full-length figure, actually and elaborately painted. There is not only this great difference in the size and finish of the picture, but it appears to have been produced on principles very different to those which govern us in our compositions. In forming our idea of a person whom we have never seen, we use chiefly our knowledge of ourselves, our acquaintance with those around us, and very often we put in some hints which have been taken from eye-witnesses. In this way we try to compose a countenance and figure which we conceive to be in harmony with a character. Masaccio and Raphael, to whose united talent we owe this portrait of the apostle, were amongst the first (as those of our readers who visited the Manchester Exhibition will remember) to escape from the conventional school that, through tradition, distorted the human body, much in the same way as the professors of theology in the time of our Lord, wrested the Scriptures. In this picture there is no trace of those vain guesses, or crude conclusions, which, entering as they do so largely into the ideal portraits of the apostle, seem to remind us of those grotesque and impossible beings which inspired the devotees of the Middle Ages.

There is no historical information about the personal appearance of the Apostle Paul. A sitting can only be obtained from his Acts and his Epistles. Any fancy portrait-painter who brings to his work a tolerably-correct acquaintance with the general rules of his art, and a special remembrance that a man who has succeeded in any arduous undertaking, is, as a law, in possession of a bodily frame in some kind of keeping with the purpose of his life, will produce, if he forgets himself and "the traditions of the elders," and draws from Scripture, a result which will, perhaps, contradict some of his former opinions.

THE CONVERSION OF SERGIUS PAULUS.   61

There is more material for an ideal portrait of the apostle than might be supposed. We have, for instance, many details about his sufferings. We can learn from those references, that he was forced by his detractors to make, to the hardships and indignities which he had endured that he must have been in the possession of a bodily frame of a very different order to the one which is popularly allotted to him.* He once and again speaks of temptations that are only known to those who possess a full physical development.† We know that he was "in labours more abundant" than any of his cotemporaries, and that these "labours" involved the possession of bodily as well as spiritual power.

These facts would lead us to accept, as probably correct, this representation of the apostle "in the flesh." We do not, however, forget that there was something in his appearance that was felt by many to be despicable, and that Paul himself was painfully aware of the unfavourable impression that his presence often produced. There is no evidence, however, that the apostle was a dwarf. We know that the apostle made "the thorn in the flesh" a matter for prayer. There are none, perhaps, who can think that he asked to have a cubit added to his stature. Raphael, by painting him in profile, seems to suggest that the face was the seat of his infirmity. It would seem that Paul never fully recovered from "the great light" which smote him to the ground at Damascus, and that some disfigurement and weakness of the eyes ever bore testimony to the fact. It might be to this that he refers, when he says, "I bear in my body the marks of the Lord Jesus."

Before turning away, we must observe one of those quiet hints of the painter, by which he is always reminding us of some point which we shall do well to notice. The book under the apostle's arm, perhaps one of those which in after years he left at Troas, seems to be only a trifle, but it is a striking index of purpose and character. Any one may see that Raphael has not studied the chronology of binding, but every one who knows Paul from his

* 2 Cor. xi. 23-28.   † 1 Cor. ix. 25-27.

Acts and his Epistles will understand that the painter would have us to remember that the apostle gave himself to reading. Those who criticise the binding of the book are likely to urge the objection of the unlikelihood of the apostle being in possession of a book, and especially at a time when he had just arrived from a long journey. It would seem that Paul, though occasionally the medium of supernatural works, never neglected the culture of his natural abilities; and while exhorting others to be diligent in the use of ordinary means, practised himself what he preached. He was a man of like feelings and passions with others. In his Acts and his Epistles we find him acting and speaking as if he were beset with the same temptations as ourselves. The book under his arm will hardly need any explanation to those who know anything of a missionary career. The apostle has felt, that being called to go about and preach everywhere, he must, at the very commencement, adopt a plan that will save him from that desultoriness of character which is apt to grow upon any who lead a wandering life.

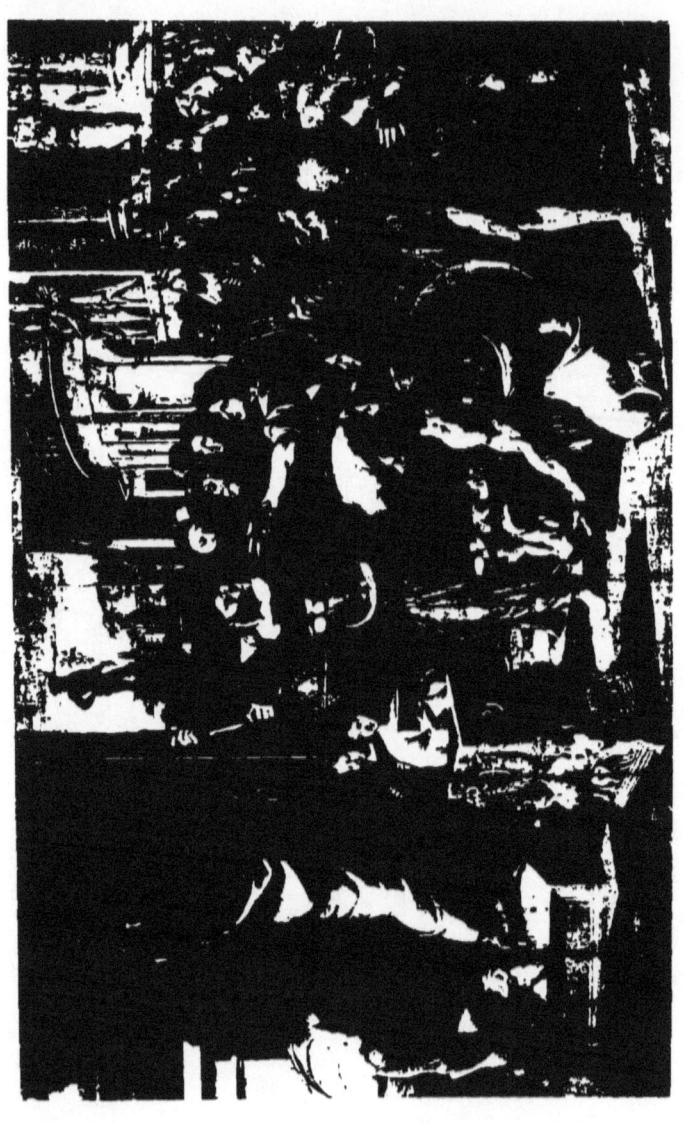

THE CARTOONS OF RAPHAEL.

No. VI.

Paul and Barnabas Rejecting the Sacrifice at Lystra.

"And it came to pass in Iconium, that they went both together into the synagogue of the Jews, and so spake, that a great multitude both of the Jews and also of the Greeks believed. But the unbelieving Jews stirred up the Gentiles, and made their minds evil affected against the brethren. Long time therefore abode they speaking boldly in the Lord, which gave testimony unto the word of his grace, and granted signs and wonders to be done by their hands. But the multitude of the city was divided: and part held with the Jews, and part with the apostles. And when there was an assault made both of the Gentiles, and also of the Jews with their rulers, to use them despitefully, and to stone them, they were aware of it, and fled unto Lystra and Derbe, cities of Lycaonia, and unto the region that lieth round about: and there they preached the gospel. And there sat a certain man at Lystra, impotent in his feet, being a cripple from his mother's womb, who never had walked: the same heard Paul speak: who steadfastly beholding him, and perceiving that he had faith to be healed, said with a loud voice, Stand upright on thy feet. And he leaped and walked. And when the people saw what Paul had done, they lifted up their voices, saying in the speech of Lycaonia, The gods are come down to us in the likeness of men. And they called Barnabas, Jupiter; and Paul, Mercurius, because he was the chief speaker. Then the priest of Jupiter, which was before their city, brought oxen and garlands unto the gates, and would have done sacrifice with the people. Which when the apostles, Barnabas and Paul, heard of, they rent their clothes, and ran in among the people, crying out, and saying, Sirs, why do ye these things? We also are men of like passions with you, and preach unto you that ye should turn from these vanities unto the living God, which made heaven, and earth, and the sea, and all things that are therein: who in times past suffered all nations to walk in their own ways. Nevertheless he left not himself without witness, in that he did good, and gave us rain from heaven, and fruitful seasons, filling our hearts with food and gladness. And with these sayings scarce restrained they the people, that they had not done sacrifice unto them. And there came thither certain Jews from Antioch and Iconium, who persuaded the people, and, having stoned Paul, drew him out of the city, supposing he had been dead. Howbeit, as the disciples stood round about him, he rose up, and came into the city: and the next day he departed with Barnabas to Derbe."
—ACTS xiv. 1-20.

PAUL AND BARNABAS REJECTING THE SACRIFICE AT LYSTRA.

"Then the priest of Jupiter, which was before their city, brought oxen and garlands unto the gates, and would have done sacrifice with the people. Which when the apostles, Barnabas and Paul, heard of, they rent their clothes."—ACTS xiv. 13, 14.

THE air of confusion which pervades this picture may be regarded as one of its chief characteristics. It is almost as distracting to look at this cartoon as it must have been to have witnessed the conflict which it represents. The whirlpool, created by the meeting of the opposite tides of feeling, bewilders, and, for the time, blinds the spectator. The masses of the Lystrians, as they pour through the streets of their ancient city, are receiving the first check to their wild and impetuous fanaticism. They stagger, and eddy, and foam under the shock. A few converts may be observed amongst the multitude; one disciple being very conspicuous, as, anticipating the mind of the apostles, he stretches over the ox, barely in time to arrest its death-blow. Paul and Barnabas are rushing out of the house, where they have been resting, in utter unconsciousness of this issue of the miracle upon the lame man. Paul meets, at the very door-step, a priest bringing a ram, and, overcome with horror, is rending his clothes. This is the moment chosen by the painter. The apostles have not yet run in amongst the people. The time is given to the instant, for you can see, by the half-lifted foot of Barnabas, that he is poising himself, having been hindered by the sudden stopping of Paul.

One other cartoon in the series produces, at first sight, a similar impression of confusion; but, in that, the spectator presently loses the distraction which, in this, seems to grow upon him as he stands and gazes. The mob that is gathering here after the healing of the heathen cripple is altogether a different assemblage to the crowd that we noticed about "the Beautiful gate," when Peter and John made the Jerusalem beggar to walk. The people who were frequenting the temple at the hour of prayer were insulated by the columns, and kept apart in all the individuality of their separate errands; and it was very evident that many of them were ignorant of the cure that was being effected. Here, however, the prodigy has been noised abroad, and the swarming multitudes press upon each other in an unbroken mass.

Raphael always laid his architecture under contribution. The suggestive associations connected with the prætorium and the conversion of Sergius Paulus,—the upper room and the sin and death of Ananias,—are only rivalled by the remarkable power with which we shall see that the painter compels the buildings around Paul, as he preaches at Athens, to tell their part in the tale. In the cartoon of "The Beautiful Gate," by the device of the pillars, Raphael has subdued the effect of confusion; here he has intensified it, by placing buildings in the background which seem half asleep with very age.

The idea of haste is also a very prominent feature in this composition. There was a reason, as will presently appear, why there should be no delay made by the Lycaonians in the acknowledgment of the appearance of their gods. The impression of hurry is given by the uplifted axe, just as the air of confusion is conveyed by the maze of intricate lines, formed by the moving figures which surge, swell, and break like the waves of a troubled sea.

The photograph, with the trick of the art, has exaggerated the chiaro-oscuro of the original, and by this manœuvre has succeeded in gaining golden opinions from embarrassed and impatient spectators. They are placed at once, unlawfully, and somewhat abruptly, in possession of the circumstances which have occasioned the tumult. Without trespassing upon their time, or giving them any trouble in asking them to think, photography, with the extravagance and unscrupulousness of popular oratory, has sacrificed truth to effect. Raphael evidently intended, by the manner in which he has treated his composition, that we should, for a time, be kept in ignorance, just as we can see that he has made it possible for us, if we are patient and thoughtful, to find out for ourselves the clue to the mystery. We are first to be sufficiently impressed with the perplexity of the scene, and then we may learn, gradually, the exact state of the case. The broken light, scattered over the whole picture, serves, as well as the fretwork of lines, to dazzle the sight and dissipate the attention; giving up ourselves to the painter, we are quickly lost in the forest of people, and we remain bewildered till our eye catches the line of the uplifted axe, which has been used by Raphael to connect the statue of Mercury with the figure of its gospel antitype; and we then understand that the servant of God and of our Lord Jesus Christ has been mistaken, by the superstitious and unsophisticated inhabitants of Lystra, for the fabled messenger of their tutelar deity.

A necessity was laid upon the photograph to reproduce the convoluted forms of the various objects; it has, however, done its best, by deepening the shadows, to deaden the distracting effect of the original, and by concentrating and heightening the light that falls upon those who are hastening and those who are interrupting the sacrifice, it gives a premature revelation of the secret. Curious and impatient listeners, in all their antipathy to thought and carelessness about truth, are only too glad to meet with any one who will pander to their vices, and will very readily absolve, from the sins of inaccuracy and overstatement, any charlatan who has studied to please them. By a happy accident, (for Fortune often favours the false,) the yellow Mercury of the original, working necessarily black in the photograph, comes forward, and forces itself upon the spectator, compelling him to notice the satisfaction with which it is receiving the homage of its devotees.

While the disciples of Raphael must be annoyed with this exaggeration and popular artifice in the photograph, they will readily perceive, and thankfully appreciate, the kindness with which it has hidden the diminutive head of the axe, and the cleverness with which it has restored the battered altar. The axe is, of course, to be regarded as the weapon of destruction, but its head, to have been effective, would have had to be much larger than it is. It was lessened by pictorial licence, much in the same way as the boats in the cartoon of "The Miraculous Draught." In the photograph, this inconsistency of size is lost in the obscurity of the shadow; and the altar, which is in a sad state of decay through time and ill-usage, has, because it was painted in monochrome, and is now nearly colourless, yielded itself up implicitly to the restorative process of the sunbeam.

The subject of this cartoon is taken, in common with "The Conversion of Sergius Paulus," from the first missionary journey of the Apostle Paul; and we shall be better able to understand the event, and to form a fairer estimate of Raphael's treatment, if we recall the intermediate history.

Paul, Barnabas, and Mark, in the true spirit of missionaries, did not stay long at Paphos; but, taking one of the small craft which lay in the harbour bound for the opposite gulf of Attaleia, they cross over to the mainland of Asia Minor, and, travelling a few miles, they arrive at Perga in Pamphylia. It would seem that the apostle is referring to this route when he is speaking to the Corinthians of "the perils of waters, and the perils of robbers," to which he had been exposed as he went about everywhere preaching the gospel. The district abounded in waterfloods, and its inhabitants added to the difficulties and dangers of travellers by their lawless and predatory habits. These toils and risks doubtless influenced Mark, and were the occasion, quite as much as any yearning after home, or any lack of hearty sympathy in the new movement, for his departure to Jerusalem.* As we see him turning back after having put his hand to the plough, we are thankful to learn, from

* Below the cartoons, as they hung in the Sistine Chapel, there were pedestal pic-

the subsequent record in the Acts and the Epistles, that he repented, and returned to the work.

Except on their way back, the apostles did not stay at Perga, but pushing their way over the rugged mountain-passes, they came upon the central table-land, and reaching Antioch in Pisidia, they worship in the synagogue of the Jews. Paul seems often to have availed himself of his rabbinical status, (for he had not been excommunicated by the Sanhedrim,) whenever he came into contact with his countrymen, much in the same way as we find him, once and again, standing upon his Roman rights. Availing himself of the opportunity afforded him by the rulers of the synagogue, he commences a discourse which bears a strong resemblance to the one delivered by Stephen before the council at Jerusalem. There is not only the same train of thought, but the same sudden change of style at the close, produced doubtless by a similar manifestation of anger and malice on the part of the Jews.

The preaching of Paul leads to the breaking up of the congregation. Most of the Jews go out of the synagogue. The proselytes remain, and beg the apostles to repeat their message the next Sabbath. Paul and Barnabas are followed, as they leave, by a mixed multitude of "Jews and religious proselytes, and speaking to them, they persuade them to continue in the grace of God." The next Sabbath, the whole city assembles, and a riot ensues. Jewish exclusiveness is exasperated by the liberalism of Christianity. The gospel is rejected by the Jews, and the apostle, shaking the responsibility of his mission to them from his soul, as he presently shakes the dust of their city from his feet, turns to the Gentiles. The envy of bigotry that led them first to contradict and blaspheme, grows into the malice of persecution, and through the influence of some of their proselytes, who were the wives of persons in authority, Paul and Barnabas are expelled out of their coasts.

Traversing the bare uplands that lie between Antioch and the

tures executed in a gold metallic colour. "The Departure of Mark" was the subject represented beneath "The Rejection of the Sacrifice at Lystra."

plain of Iconium, the apostles preach in the synagogue of that city, and so speak, that a great multitude, both of the Jews and the Greeks also believe. "But the unbelieving Jews stirred up the Gentiles, and made their minds evil affected against the brethren." The former persecution is repeated. The contest is, however, prolonged in this instance, and many signs and wonders are granted as a Divine testimony to the mission. The whole city becomes interested. At first there is a schism—"part holding with the Jews, and part with the apostles." At last there is an assault, and the apostles, to escape death by stoning, are compelled to flee.

Paul and Barnabas now retire into a wilder region, and coming to Lystra, a city of Lycaonia, they find themselves amongst a people comparatively untouched either by Jewish prejudice or Roman civilisation.

There was no synagogue at Lystra, and its rude and credulous population retained their belief in the traditions, and their use of the dialect of their ancestors. At Paphos, the apostles had preached where the Cyprian goddess had first landed when she rose from the sea; they are now where, as the legend ran, Jupiter had once appeared in human shape, and had visited Lycaon, a king of Arcadia. The people were prepared to offer the god divine honours, but they were prevented from doing so by Lycaon, who was metamorphosed by the enraged deity into a wolf.

Having no synagogue as a starting point, the proceedings of the apostles would be somewhat altered, and they must have adopted the plan that is common amongst modern missionaries, and have entered into conversation in the streets with bystanders, and those passengers whom they could persuade to stop and listen to them. While, however, there was no place of Jewish worship in Lystra, there was a Jewish family. One of its inhabitants had married a Jewess, and the woman, with her mother and son, were living in this outlandish city when Paul came there preaching the gospel. The sacred historian, in one of those verses in which much time is contained in a very few words, refers to the fact that some interval elapsed before the incident occurred which is represented in this cartoon. It is probable that it was during this period that Paul first became acquainted with Lois, Eunice, and Timothy. The necessary isolation in which this family would live,—far removed from all their past hallowed associations, and shut out from anything like friendly social contact with their neighbours,—would dispose them, in a measure, to receive with favour the strange tidings of their countryman; and a remembrance of the fact will serve somewhat to explain the strong personal regard the apostle had for them, and his high estimate of their unfeigned faith. They are not the last exiles who have been given as seals to missionaries, nor are they the only believers whose faith has owed much of its purity and power to the solitude of a foreign land. Raphael appears, as we shall see, to have supposed that they had become believers before the miracle was wrought upon the cripple.

It was while preaching at Lystra, in some place of public resort, that the attention of Paul was attracted by a certain man impotent in his feet, being a cripple from his mother's womb. The lame man had been listening with a faith that betrayed itself in his countenance. He seems to have argued—inferring from the love of God to all, the love of God to him—inferring from the power of God over the soul, the power of God over the body. The expression of his face interrupts the apostle, who leaves off speaking, and for a moment stays steadfastly scrutinising the features of the believer. By the light of a divine physiognomy, he reads that the man has faith to be healed; and by an impulse within, he finds that the lame man has pleased God, and that it is His will "that it shall be to him according to his faith." With a loud voice, the effect of the sudden inspiration, he bids the cripple, who has till now done nothing more than creep, to stand upright on his feet. The faith of the man saves him. He stands—and leaps—and walks.

For aught that the apostle says to the contrary, the spectators of the miracle would imagine that by his own power and holiness he has made the man to walk.

The fact of the cure is told in the cartoon with admirable tact. We are assured of the truth by an eye-witness. Raphael has introduced in the left-hand corner a group of four figures, whose business it is to explain the present by the past. They tell their tale well. The man who was lame, standing with his foot between the crutches, (that now lie useless on the ground,) is evidently lost in adoring gratitude. His face, bearing the indelible marks of the class of patients to which he has for such a length of time belonged, glows with an expression of his indescribable feelings. He is utterly unconscious of the inspection that is taking place. In his ecstasy, he raises and clasps his hands, and gazes upon Paul. An elderly man, with an air that convinces us at once of his trustworthiness and respectability, is gently lifting the border of the garment, so that the unclothed limb stands fully revealed. He does this in a manner which shews that he is conscious that he is taking a liberty which the circumstance of the case would alone justify. It is possible that he may be the Greek, the father of Timothy. The two others are attempting to avail themselves of this rare opportunity of obtaining ocular demonstration of the fact which has caused such sudden and extraordinary excitement in their city.

The effect of the cure upon the citizens was terrific. The Jews, under similar circumstances, had been ready to attribute Divine power to Peter and John, although Peter had distinctly prefaced his address to the beggar with the words, "In the name of Jesus of Nazareth." The Lystrians, hearing nothing to contradict the notion, conceive the apostles to be gods, and believing in their divine nature, prepared to offer them Divine worship. Living as they did in a city that was under the special tutelage of Jupiter, having also a temple dedicated to him at the very gates, which had been founded in commemoration of a most memorable manifestation in former ages—still holding most implicitly those delusions which were becoming obsolete in the more refined and sceptical circles of heathendom—swayed by their faith—remembering how their forefathers had perished through unbelief—they rend the air with their cries,

"The gods are come down in the likeness of men. And they called Barnabas Jupiter, and Paul Mercurius, because he was the chief speaker."

The news spreads, for it is published in the native dialect. The language that reveals their notion to their fellow-citizens hides it from the apostles. Paul and Barnabas must have received the terrible tidings from some converts. Meanwhile, the priest of Jupiter hastens to give official form and power to the popular phrensy, "and bringing oxen and garlands to the gates, would have done sacrifice with the people."

Raphael has laid the scene where it doubtless occurred, not at the gates of the city, but, in accordance with the term used in the original text, at the gate or vestibule, which gave admission from the public street into the court of the house in which the apostles were staying.

He is said to have taken his representation of a heathen sacrifice from an ancient bas-relief. There seems to be some reason to believe that he did so. It is a pity that he had no better authority for his information. The small altar, the drooping head of the victim that is in the act of being slaughtered, the downward look of the priest who is about to strike its death-blow, (with an axe, instead of a knife,) are all out of keeping with the orthodox method. After looking at his copy, we are reminded of those groundless charges of plagiarism which are ever being preferred against the greatest authors. In the ancient sculpture, there are indeed two oxen with the priests and the various attendants, all crowned with bay leaves; but there is little else in it that would remind any one of the painter's obligation. Each of the figures has been cast in the same expressionless mould. The priest with the axe is unfortunately standing in such a position, that if it were conceivable that he could ever move, he would grievously damage several of his companions, and, apparently, strike the ox at which he is not aiming.

In the cartoon, you can tell, by the position of the hands, that the priest has this very moment swung up the axe. He is interrupted by a young disciple, who stretches out his arm just in time. In another moment the hands would have been brought together, (as they are found in the bas-relief,) and the interference would have been too late. No one then could have stayed the blow. This opportune service is supposed to have been rendered by Timothy, perhaps at the quick-witted suggestion of a woman, for there is a female figure introduced at his side, which may be taken, because of the resemblance, for his mother.

The quietness of the two aged priests who stand absorbed in devotion, one having his brow bound with the sacred fillet, together with the official routine of the three attendants, who are half-kneeling in a row by the side of the ox, form a strong contrast to the energy of their companion, and to the excitement of the mob. This effect is increased by the two children at the altar, both marvellous pictures of juvenile perfunctoriness; the one is carrying the box of sacrificial flour, the other is piping to his heart's content.

A close observation will enable the spectator to detect an alteration which Raphael has made in the figure which is holding the victim. In the drawing made for the cartoon of "The Charge to Peter," we saw that, upon second thoughts, the painter deviated from his first plan in the disposition of the drapery on the figure of our Lord. Here, the alteration can be traced on the very cartoon. At first, the man held the horn with his left hand; but he has now a better purchase, having hold of both those points which will give him power over the ox, should it struggle. By this exchange, Raphael lost an angle and gained a curve. A similar instance may be discovered in the hand of the figure of our Lord in "The Miraculous Draught."

Tidings have reached the apostles. Rushing out of the house, they are seen for a moment upon the steps. In another instant, Paul will have turned, allowing Barnabas room to move—and they will run in amongst the people, and endeavour to arrest their proceedings by a few well-chosen, burning words. Their actions would speak more loudly than anything they could say. They place themselves on the same level as the people. They shew by deeds, as well as say by words, that they are but men. Trembling with shame, wild with horror, they are in the midst of the mob with rent clothes, heated earnestness, and excited speech. The Lystrians can see for themselves that they are not passionless deities, but men of like feelings and passions with themselves.

Happily, bitter bigots bent upon the destruction of Paul arrive at this crisis. They crowd around the attendants who have the second ox in charge, and, availing themselves of the vindictiveness of disappointment, the scene that occurred in the streets of Jerusalem before the crucifixion of our Lord is repeated in the city of Lystra. The mob turns upon the apostles, headed by women and men breathing threatening and slaughter. Barnabas escapes. The stones of the streets are torn up, and the barbarous Lystrians, led by the bloodthirsty Jews, bear down upon Paul. It must have been with him one of those moments in which thought and feeling acquire supernatural clearness, force, and velocity. He falls; in the same instant, realising that the measure he had meted out to others is about to be measured to him—living over again the stoning of Stephen—conscious that he has obtained mercy—and thankful that, instead of being worshipped, he is only stoned by the people.

THE CARTOONS OF RAPHAEL.

No. VII.

Paul Preaching at Athens.

"But when the Jews of Thessalonica had knowledge that the word of God was preached of Paul at Berea, they came thither also, and stirred up the people. And then immediately the brethren sent away Paul to go as it were to the sea: but Silas and Timotheus abode there still. And they that conducted Paul brought him unto Athens: and receiving a commandment unto Silas and Timotheus for to come to him with all speed, they departed. Now while Paul waited for them at Athens, his spirit was stirred in him, when he saw the city wholly given to idolatry. Therefore disputed he in the synagogue with the Jews, and with the devout persons, and in the market daily with them that met with him. Then certain philosophers of the Epicureans, and of the Stoicks, encountered him. And some said, What will this babbler say? other some, He seemeth to be a setter forth of strange gods: because he preached unto them Jesus, and the resurrection. And they took him, and brought him unto Areopagus, saying, May we know what this new doctrine, whereof thou speakest, is? For thou bringest certain strange things to our ears: we would know therefore what these things mean. (For all the Athenians and strangers which were there spent their time in nothing else, but either to tell, or to hear some new thing.) Then Paul stood in the midst of Mars' hill, and said, Ye men of Athens, I perceive that in all things ye are too superstitious. For as I passed by, and beheld your devotions, I found an altar with this inscription, TO THE UNKNOWN GOD. Whom therefore ye ignorantly worship, him declare I unto you. God, that made the world and all things therein, seeing that he is Lord of heaven and earth, dwelleth not in temples made with hands; neither is worshipped with men's hands, as though he needed anything, seeing he giveth to all life, and breath, and all things; and hath made of one blood all nations of men for to dwell on all the face of the earth, and hath determined the times before appointed, and the bounds of their habitation; that they should seek the Lord, if haply they might feel after him, and find him, though he be not far from every one of us : for in him we live, and move, and have our being; as certain also of your own poets have said, For we are also his offspring. Forasmuch then as we are the offspring of God, we ought not to think that the Godhead is like unto gold, or silver, or stone, graven by art and man's device. And the times of this ignorance God winked at; but now commandeth all men everywhere to repent : because he hath appointed a day, in the which he will judge the world in righteousness by that man whom he hath ordained ; whereof he hath given assurance unto all men, in that he hath raised him from the dead. And when they heard of the resurrection of the dead, some mocked : and others said, We will hear thee again of this matter. So Paul departed from among them. Howbeit certain men clave unto him, and believed ; among the which was Dionysius the Areopagite, and a woman named Damaris, and others with them."—ACTS xvii. 13-34.

PAUL PREACHING AT ATHENS.

"And when they heard of the resurrection of the dead, some mocked: and others said, We will hear thee again of this matter. So Paul departed from among them. Howbeit certain men clave unto him, and believed: among the which was Dionysius the Areopagite, and a woman named Damaris."—ACTS xvii. 32-34.

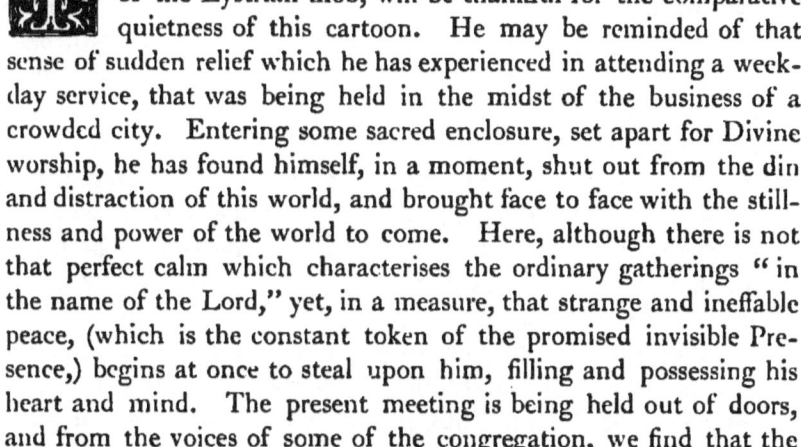HE spectator, as he turns away from the confusion and riot of the Lystrian mob, will be thankful for the comparative quietness of this cartoon. He may be reminded of that sense of sudden relief which he has experienced in attending a week-day service, that was being held in the midst of the business of a crowded city. Entering some sacred enclosure, set apart for Divine worship, he has found himself, in a moment, shut out from the din and distraction of this world, and brought face to face with the stillness and power of the world to come. Here, although there is not that perfect calm which characterises the ordinary gatherings " in the name of the Lord," yet, in a measure, that strange and ineffable peace, (which is the constant token of the promised invisible Presence,) begins at once to steal upon him, filling and possessing his heart and mind. The present meeting is being held out of doors, and from the voices of some of the congregation, we find that the usual licence of open-air services has been taken. A knot of persons are discussing amongst themselves the statements which they have heard.

The upright figure of the preacher, who has enchained the greater part of his audience in wrapt attention; the multitude of parallel perpendicular lines in the various buildings; the harmony of colour; the large proportion of unoccupied space which has been reserved for Paul; his impassioned utterance; and the circle which the people have formed as they stand around him, all combine to suggest the earnestness and tranquillity which seem to be essential and peculiar to Christian worship.

This cartoon completed the original series, and while it is to be regretted that time and chance have stolen away three of the intermediate cartoons, it is a satisfaction to find that they have spared the first and the last. The unity of the painter's purpose, though somewhat marred by the loss of the missing cartoons, is still apparent, being easily discovered in those which remain.

Losses are seldom without profits. Through the absence of the cartoon of "The Imprisonment at Philippi," the scene at Lystra is brought into juxtaposition with "The Sermon at Athens," and by this accident the apostle is portrayed, in a pair of pictures, presenting the gospel, in the one case, to those whose faith in heathenism had been shaken, and, in the other, to those who were still heathens in deed and in truth.

The three cartoons in which the subjects are taken from the career of the apostle of the Gentiles, form a triad, representing three conflicts of Christianity. At Paphos, there is a contest with the kingdom of darkness. At Lystra, there is a renewal of hostilities with religious bigotry. At Athens, the struggle is inaugurated between reason and faith.

Including the two other events which belong to the Book of the Acts, there is a further and fuller manifestation of the antagonism of the gospel, as it comes into contact with natural deformity and natural depravity. Or, leaving the cartoon of "The Healing of the Lame Beggar," and the cartoon of "The Hypocrite," to form a pair by themselves, there is in them the earnest of our redemption from all evil; the prophecy of that land where "the inhabitants shall not say, I am sick," and where "there shall in no wise enter anything that defileth, neither whatsoever worketh abomination, or maketh a lie."

In the whole series of the seven, (remembering that in them all there is the representation of the acts of our Redeemer, either before His death, after His resurrection, or since His ascension,) we have " Jesus Christ the same yesterday, to-day, and for ever," manifesting the almighty power, the infinite mercy, the overruling providence, and the just judgment of God. Our Lord is, by them all, evidently set forth. In " The Miraculous Draught," revealing the Father. In " The Charge to Peter," reproving and pardoning sin. At " The Beautiful Gate," redeeming the body. In " The Upper Room," dooming the hypocrite. In "The Blinding of Elymas," defeating the work of the devil. At Lystra, making the wrath of man to praise Him. And at Athens, casting down imaginations, and every high thing that exalteth itself against the knowledge of God.

Paul preached at Athens during his second missionary journey, and it will be necessary to resume the thread of his history, in order to sympathise with the apostle in the new position in which we here find him. A recollection of intervening events, and some acquaintance with the Athenians of the time, is due to the painter before considering his treatment of this scene. We left Paul in the hands of the murderous mob at Lystra, who having, as they thought, effected their purpose, drew him out of the city supposing that he had been dead. He was " cast down, but not destroyed." Immortal till his work was done, he rises up, as the disciples stand around him; and the next day, with the perseverance of a true saint, and in the spirit of a true missionary, departs to Derbe. The apostles, after preaching in this city, retrace their steps, and braving, with their Master's courage, the danger of a return, make their way homeward, revisiting Lystra, Iconium, and Antioch, " confirming the souls of the disciples, and exhorting them to continue in the faith, and that we must through much tribulation enter into the kingdom of God."

It was during a temporary rest from their missionary labour that the discussion of a subject, (which had become the topic of the day,) was forced upon the apostles. The question was fairly raised by the arrival of Judaizers at the free Church of Antioch, who insisted upon the necessity of circumcision to salvation. This was formally debated by a council at Jerusalem. The narrative of the whole proceedings is not only deeply interesting, as a manifestation of the condition and conduct of the early Church, but it is also of great importance in the information it supplies respecting the difficulties of the position of the apostle Paul, and the light which it throws upon his separation from Barnabas.

The point in dispute was not the relation of the *gospel*, but the relation of the *law* to the Gentiles. Jewish prejudice had been obliged, by the vision of Peter, to concede that the blessings of the gospel were to be shared with the Gentiles; it was now fighting hard to burden them with the requirements of the Mosaic law. At first, as was to be expected, there was no small dissension and disputation. The controversy led to the appointment of a deputation from the Church at Antioch, including Paul and Barnabas, to the Church at Jerusalem. Paul describes his feelings and conduct at this time in his letter to the Galatians, and the second chapter of that epistle should be studied in connexion with the fifteenth chapter of the Book of the Acts.

It would appear that, after some preliminary interviews with the apostles and with the Church, a general meeting was called. The meeting opened with considerable confusion, the most insignificant and, not unlikely, the most troublesome speaking first. Peter at last rose, and secured silence by a short and striking speech. He met with universal deference, because of his peculiar claim to be heard upon the matter in hand. He referred to the fact, that the question had been settled long since by Divine interference; that the same purifying Spirit had been poured out upon the Gentiles as upon themselves; and that they had already confessed that there was no salvation by the law, but only through the grace of our Lord Jesus Christ. Paul and Barnabas then related the story of their recent enterprise, referring not only to the free gospel which they had preached, but to the conversions and the miracles that had accompanied their mission. James then suggested a practical conclusion, which was unanimously adopted, and the deputation returned, bearing a written document, and accompanied by "Barnabas and Silas, chief men among the brethren." In the letter, the Church at Jerusalem disowned any connexion with the Judaizing party; acknowledged the Christian worth of Barnabas and Paul; and recommended abstaining from certain practices common amongst the heathen.

It might have been expected that this formal settlement of the question would have been final, and that the middle wall of partition would have been entirely broken down. Peter, however, comes to Antioch, and led astray by his fears denies, by his conduct, the statement he had made in the council at Jerusalem. Barnabas is carried away with his dissimulation. Paul is obliged publicly to withstand the influence of Peter, and to expose the blameworthiness of his conduct. After a while, (perhaps to allow Barnabas time to recover himself,) Paul proposes to his former missionary colleague that they should revisit the scenes of their labours. Barnabas makes the company of Mark a condition. Paul objects to Mark as unsuitable. The uncle, a man of great kindness, as may be proved from the sale of his property, and his patronage of Paul when no one believed in him, would easily forgive the defection of the nephew, and readily afford him a fresh trial. He would also (for Mark was a member of the Jerusalem Church) find his relative somewhat likeminded with himself upon the vexed question of the day. Paul knew, however, that a full and complete conviction of the perfect liberty of the gospel was imperatively required in those who came into contact with the heathen converts; and that fickle men were not to be intrusted with difficult duty. The difference of opinion led to a division of labour. Barnabas and Mark sailed to Cyprus. Paul chose for his companion Silas, a man in the same social position as himself, " being a Roman," and holding similar convictions of the freeness and sufficiency of the gospel.

The subject of the third lost cartoon is taken from the second missionary journey of Paul, representing an event which is recorded at unusual length in the sacred history, and which has only to be carefully considered, and we shall perceive the special importance of the narrative, and the profound spiritual insight of the painter. The record seems to have been written for our learning, that we, through patience and comfort of this scripture, might have hope in God as the Hearer and the Answerer of prayer.

Paul and Silas having visited the churches in Syria and Cilicia, and enlisted the services of Timothy at Lystra, are brought before us attempting to break new ground. They are at their wits' end. Forbidden by the Holy Ghost to preach in proconsular Asia, they travel on towards Mysia, and there, attempting to turn northwards to Bithynia, they are again arrested by a Divine impulse. Journeying eastwards, (the only direction in which they are not interrupted,) they at last reach the port of Troas. Meantime some women had been praying without ceasing on the banks of the small stream Gangites, which ran by the Macedonian city of Philippi. The humble prayer-meeting was evidently connected with the supernatural direction of the movements of the missionaries. Paul and his companions are led by the Hearer and Answerer of prayer to the place where prayer was wont to be made.

It is not surprising, after this remarkable instance of the power of prayer, that Paul and Silas are to be found, in the same night after they had been shamefully entreated at Philippi, praying. Raphael has chosen this midnight scene as one of his subjects. Behind the grating of the prison, the apostle is to be seen in prayer, and, in strict harmony with the narrative, the earthquake is represented as cotemporaneous. This instance of faith is identical with that on the part of Hezekiah, of which we have a threefold record. It is to such cases as these that the promise applies, "And it shall come to pass, that before they call, I will answer, and while they are yet speaking, I will hear."

Time would fail us, if we attempted to explore further this mine of events. We turn away, only asking the reader to study the first

Epistle to the Thessalonians, in connexion with the history of the mission to Thessalonica and Berea.

Paul, again a refugee, leaving behind him Silas and Timothy at Berea, has been hurried away from the reach of his persecutors. The brethren who had aided his flight, and had accompanied him as far as the Piræus, have been dismissed with a message to his fellow-labourers in the gospel to come to him with all speed, and the apostle is left at Athens alone.

It will be almost as difficult to understand the feelings of Paul, as he tarried at Athens, as it is to appreciate his sermon. The apostle, notwithstanding appearances to the contrary, was a man of great social feeling. Obliged to separate from "his brethren according to the flesh," his heart yet yearned strangely after them.* Called to witness to a truth, and to adopt a line of conduct which was very unacceptable to most of his brethren in Christ, he is constantly, in his letters, regretting his loneliness.† Many a passage in the Book of the Acts, and many a reference in the various epistles might be quoted, proving that the most isolated of the apostles was "not a whit behind the very chiefest," in the greatest of the Christian graces. This disposition will account for the fact, to which prominence is given by Luke, and to which the apostle himself refers in his first letter to the Thessalonians, that he felt it to be a burden and a grief to be left at Athens alone.

There is in Raphael's portrait of the preacher, notwithstanding his excitement, a lonesomeness lingering over his face and his figure, which reminds us of the lamentation, "I have trodden the winepress alone, and of the people there was none with me."

Timothy appears to have obeyed the summons of Paul, and after having arrived at Athens, to have been sent back again to Thessalonica.‡ Only those who have felt the loneliness of great cities will be able, in any measure, to sympathise with the apostle, as he lives on, day after day, depressed with a sense of solitude, in the midst of a multitude of people. Only those who have anxiously trod the

* Rom. ix. 1–3, x. 1.   † 2 Tim. iv. 10–16.   ‡ 1 Thess. iii. 1.

streets of a city, pressed in spirit with a necessity that has been laid upon them to preach the gospel, are at all likely to form any conception of the working of the mind of the apostle, as he attempts to win a hearing for truths, which he knows will only excite disgust or ridicule. No citizen of the world would ever be able to read the heart of this stranger. No popular preacher could believe in the travail of his soul. The cartoon was not painted either for those who are always at home in the pulpit, or for those who can be at home in their travels, in any place and with any people.

The architecture is not intended to be a literal representation of the buildings which were around Paul as he stood upon the Areopagus. The painter will grievously disappoint any who, having studied some of the numerous hand-books and guides to Athens, expect to find in Raphael the detail and preciseness of pre-Raphaelitism. Had he chosen, the painter might have easily reproduced " Mars' Hill in the Time of the Roman Empire;" for he had in his pay, travelling artists, whom he used to send throughout Italy and Greece, to make studies for his pictures. He had here, however, a subject which would only have become commonplace, if he had descended to the pedantry of prose. He gave himself up, and specially in his treatment of the architecture, to the power of poetry.

He has, first, nearly enclosed the whole scene with idolatrous edifices, only leaving two narrow outlets, and even through them fresh views are obtained of the city, in which every public building had its religious associations. The oppressive nearness of the idol temples, with the heavy gloom of the shadows which are resting upon them, distress and darken the mind of the spectator, till he is somewhat relieved by a comparatively high and warm light shining upon the broken arch which partially overhangs the preacher.

The mystery that has hung about this broken arch may perhaps be thus explained. The keystone of heathenism, (at any rate, in the most intelligent circles of heathendom,) had given way. Educated people had lost their faith in their religion. They still made a profession of idolatry, but it was no longer in power, but only in form. Any one might see from their works, that though they had a name that they lived, they were dead.

In this city, which, in the time of Paul, might be compared with modern Rome, the apostle, not giving way to the morbid inaction of the sorrow of the world, but braced by godly sorrow for the duty of the day, breaks ground, first by reasoning with the Jews in their synagogue, and then by arguing in the Agora with the Athenians who had embraced Judaism. This plan of public disputation was evidently adapted to excite the interest of the idlers, who frequented, for mere gossip, the scene of past glorious memories. He appears, according to his invariable custom, to have been insisting upon the fact of the resurrection of our Lord, and being overheard by followers of the two philosophical sects that yet retained some vitality, he was invited by them, partly in derision and partly in curiosity, to deliver a discourse.

Raphael has not represented Paul in the act of pleading before a tribunal, but, most distinctly, in the act of preaching. The hill of Areopagus had been indeed the scene of a long series of awful causes, connected with crime and religion, beginning with the legendary trial of Mars, which gave to the place the name of Mars' Hill.* There is, however, nothing in the record which would lead us to suppose that Paul was placed on his defence, and there is no trace of a trial in the cartoon. Instead of the judges sitting upon seats hewn out in the rock, and the accuser and the criminal standing on the rough stones, (which, according to Euripides, were assigned to them,) there is in the gathering, the well-known aspect that is common to all congregations who are listening to a sermon.

Sixteen stone stairs cut in the rock, at its south-east angle, lead up to the hill of the Areopagus from the valley of the Agora, which lies between it and the Pnyx. The solemnity of the place was increased by the neighbourhood of the Temple of Mars, and the sanctuary of the Eumenides. Raphael suggests these recollections by his flight of steps, his sombre buildings, and his statue of the god of war.

* Pausanias, xxviii. 5.

The apostle stands like a pillar. This similitude is evidently the key to much of the meaning of the picture. The comparison is suggested by the repeated alliteration of lines formed by the columns of the temples, and is indicated still more clearly by the pillar which has been curiously introduced above the head of Paul, and of which his body may be conceived to be the continuation. The idea originated by form is sustained by colour. The complementary green marble of the columns attracts and cools the eye, which has been riveted by the blazing drapery of the apostle.

By faith Paul stands, and stands alone. He is not merely the only believer in the midst of those who were staggering through unbelief, but he was the only Christian of his day who acted as if he believed in the last command of our Lord. The apostle was the main support of the missionary movement, and he was left to stand as much alone in the Church as he did in the world.

The congregation is small. As a working man lately said to us, "He has not got many to hear him." There might have been more present at the beginning of the sermon, for we can see some that are now going away. The apostle is represented as having reached that point, so distressing to a preacher, where he has given a fearless utterance to a truth, which has enraged (as he had expected) the greater part of his audience. In the agony of his earnestness, he has unconsciously worked his way to the very brink of the step, as if he would have imparted to the people not only the gospel of God, but his own soul also. In another moment or two, the under-tone of argument, which we distinguished as we came up to look and to listen, will have broken out into open mockery. At first, because the younger men are evidently the more hopeful portion of the congregation, it might be supposed that the two young men who are sitting near the disputants and turning round toward them, are attempting to silence the indecent interruption. They are, we are afraid, being led away by their seniors.

Before the congregation breaks up, we may take the opportunity of looking round, and attempt to estimate the varied feelings. We must be guided wholly by our physiognomical instincts, for only two in the congregation are personally known to us. On the one side, at the right, are the most hopeful; on the other side, at the left, are the most hopeless.

The three figures behind Paul, two of which we can hardly see for the darkness, may be taken to represent Jews. Each of them bears the mark of his residence in a foreign land. All of them have the look of beasts of prey, and shrinking from the gaze of the apostle, they seem to have chosen their dark corner, slinking away at his back, as evil-doers who hated the light. The corpulent fellow, with those lines of pain in his sensual face, which are often to be seen in those who are in subjection to their body, may remind spectators who have studied Holman Hunt's picture, of the burly doctor of the law in "The Finding of Christ in the Temple." His neighbour with the unshorn locks and the solemn beard is evidently one of those religious impostors of the day, who lived upon the shipwrecks of faith, which were constantly occurring. The third man, who has seated himself on the corner of the top step, is a fair sample of the stiff-necked race to which he belongs. In neither of these three is there the slightest trace of religious or philosophic interest.

The difference in the ages of the audience is very conspicuous. The young men, with the exception of the two already noticed, stand together in an outer circle. Most of them have not formed any opinion for themselves. Some, as we have seen, will side with those who cavil; others will draw off with those who wish to hear again of the matter.

The knot of elder men, who are now becoming heated with argument, are enveloped in darkness by the photograph, and appear in the original as sadly-faded specimens of Stoics and Epicureans. As it happens, these figures are found, in this otherwise well-preserved cartoon, in a very damaged position. These accidents are very suggestive. They may serve to remind us of the cloudiness and the confusion which generally attend all disputation. There is also a striking analogy between the change wrought by centuries upon the cartoon since it was first painted, and the demoralisation of the sects since the days of their founders.

The three men who stand immediately in front of the preacher can be as easily distinguished from each other in the photograph by the expression of their countenances, as they may be in the original by the colour of their clothes. There is the same aid called in here by the painter as we noticed in the group of the apostles in "The Charge to Peter." They are not, perhaps, to be regarded as exponents of particular schools of philosophy. Raphael, it may be conceived, has represented the surviving power of the Porch and the Garden in the group of debaters, and in the scorner who stands behind the youngest of these three listeners. The first man is in middle life, and as he lifts up his open, candid face, you see that the seed is falling into good ground. He is hearing the word with an honest and good heart.

The old man leaning on the crutch is not now listening. His inattention to the sermon may be the result of pain, for his face and half-lifted foot betoken suffering. Or, what is more probable, —for, with such a forehead as he has, he must often have reflected upon men and things,—he is endeavouring to form an estimate of the apostle, and he does not allow his scrutiny to be disturbed by listening to what he says. Familiar as he must have been with the pride of the impassive Stoic, and the vanity of the pleasure-loving Epicurean, he has toiled up the hill to see more of a man whose conduct was even more remarkable than his creed. He is evidently puzzled with the display of Christian earnestness and Christian love.

The figure with his chin resting on his breast is lost in thought. He has been listening, but he is now debating with himself the conclusiveness of the arguments of the apostle. He has folded his arms, and his hands are hidden in his mantle; so that we are, at first, somewhat reminded of his neighbour who is receiving the truth in the love of it. There is, however, all the difference between them. In the one case, the arms have been folded; but they have been gradually relaxed as the man has gradually given up himself to believe what he hears. His arms are now drooping, and if we could see his hands, we should discover them to be open. In this instance, we should find the hands clenched. The different angle at the elbow bespeaks the resistance to the force of truth. The brow belongs to a logician. He is testing the logic of the sermon. You can see that he is not hearing what Paul is now declaring about the resurrection of our Lord. He is weighing the three statements that the apostle had previously made respecting the worship of God.

There are now but two of the congregation whom we have not noticed, and we have only to look at them, and we shall feel that it would have been worth while to have endured a far greater amount of agony and shame, as the price of their reception of the truth. They are evidently believers. Their joy is the test of their faith. They not only believe, but they " also joy in God through our Lord Jesus Christ, by whom they have now received the atonement." Their names are connected in the sacred record, and they are placed together in the cartoon. They have been brought by the preaching of Paul into the same fellowship. A little while ago, there could not, perhaps, have been found, in all Athens, two persons between whom there was a wider gulf of separation. The woman is supposed to have been an *hetæra*. The seclusion of the Greek women in respectable life renders her presence in the crowd on the Areopagus very suspicious. The mention of her name by Luke would suggest the idea that there was something remarkable in her conversion. Other persons were converted under this sermon besides Damaris and Dionysius, but we can easily understand why their names should have been passed over in silence, and prominence given to the fact, that an Areopagite and a woman of the town were amongst the first-fruits of the gospel at Athens.

Dionysius appears as if he would ascend the stairs to meet Paul. He opens his arms and hands, as if he desired not only to receive the faith, but also to embrace the person of the apostle. A member of the most august assembly in the world, among the first politicians and orators of his day, sprung from the noblest blood of Greece, he is one of the wise, and rich, and noble, who entered with publicans and harlots into the kingdom of God.

There is reason to believe, from the hardness in some of the faces, and the absence of detail in the extremities and drapery, that Raphael left a large portion of this cartoon to be finished by his disciples. He reserved, however, to himself the apostle and his converts. His hand may be traced in the countenance of Dionysius, and his initials can be read on the drapery that is thrown over the shoulder of Damaris.

This cartoon is the most popular of the seven, and its popularity may be attributed partly to the plainness of the subject and the simplicity of its treatment; partly to its harmony of colour, and the comparatively high state of its preservation.

We have lingered already too long over this last cartoon. We turn away from expounding the photographs, much in the same mood as we left the gallery after we had completed our copies of the originals. In neither case have we spared time or labour, but in neither case have we attained success. We have done what we could, and we know what could yet be done. We will not, however, keep our readers waiting to hear what we have to say now our " occupation 's gone." We cheer ourselves with the hope, that, as many have been led to the gallery, by our copies, to see for themselves the precious relics of Raphael's genius, so more may be induced by our expositions to study those records from which he derived his inspiration.

Ballantyne & Company, Printers, Edinburgh.

www.ingramcontent.com/pod-product-compliance
Lightning Source LLC
Chambersburg PA
CBHW020124170426
43199CB00009B/630